The Art of Drama, v

Romeo & Juliet

PERIPETEIA PRESS

Published by Peripeteia Press Ltd.

First published November 2020

ISBN: 978-1-913577-02-5

Contents

Introduction to *The Art of Drama* series

The German philosopher Nietzsche described his work as 'the greatest gift that [mankind] has ever been given'. The Elizabethan poet Edmund Spenser hoped his book *The Faerie Queene* would magically transform readers into noblemen. In comparison, our aims for The Art of Drama series of books are a little more modest. Fundamentally we aim to provide books that will be of maximum use to students of English and to their teachers. In our experience, few GCSE students read essays on literary texts, yet, whatever specification they are studying, they have to produce their own analytical essays. So, we're offering some models, written in a lively and accessible, but also scholarly style.

In this series of books, we aim to reproduce the success of our *The Art of Poetry* series by providing fine-grained, well-informed and engaging material on the key issues in key drama set texts. In the first book in the series, we focused on J. B. Priestley's popular old stager, *An Inspector Calls*. In the second in our series, we turned our critical attention to Shakespeare's notoriously dark and troubling Scottish play, *Macbeth*. In third we explored perhaps the bard's most famous play, *Hamlet*, and in this edition we turn to another of his most celebrated and studied plays, *Romeo and Juliet*.

As with all our poetry books, we hope this new series will appeal to English teachers as well as students of Literature. However, there is a plethora of material already available on Shakespeare's plays on the market. Many books aimed at GCSE pupils present information in condensed, broken up or broken down, note and bullet pointed formats. In contrast, a distinguishing feature of our critical guides is that they are organized as a series of short essays. We ask students to write essays, yet rarely before A-level do we encourage them to read literary essays, not least because there's a paucity of this sort of academic material pitched at this age group. Hence we have tried to fill this significant gap with essays modelling how to engage critically with Literary texts.

With the seemingly ever-increasing demands and importance of terminal exams, there's a great pressure on students and their teachers to reach top grades. One way to attempt to do this is to drill students with exam techniques and fill their heads with information in the hope that they will be able to regurgitate it accurately in examinations. To us, that sort of approach cuts out the essential parts of the experience of reading and writing about literature, perhaps the most rewarding and richest parts of the experience, i.e. developing our own critical views. Good critical writing about poems, novels and plays does not merely repeat somebody else's ideas; rather it expresses the critical opinions of the writer, informed, of course, by their experiences in the classroom and elsewhere. No two essays on any Literary text should say exactly the same things. Ideally teaching should nurture pupils' ability to express their own critical thinking about texts in their own emerging critical voices, informed as we say by discussion with peers and the expertise of teachers.

Our essays in this collection do not follow any specific framework or aim to hit any specific assessment objectives for any specific exam. We are not trying to get in 12.5% of context or to make sure we always finish with a resonant quote. Rather the writers of this guide have been given the freedom to write about what they find most interesting about their chosen topic, whether this be a central theme, character or scene. It is our conviction that when we write about the things that most interest we us we write our best work.

Our GCSE books aim to inspire and enrich the literary experiences of pupils aiming for level 7 or thereabouts and above, though we hope they will be useful for all students of Literature.

Writing about plays

The play and the novel

Plays and novels have several significant features in common, such as characters, dialogue, plots and settings. In addition, pupils read plays in lessons, often sitting at desks in the same way as they study novels. So it's not surprising that many pupils treat these two related, but distinct, literary art forms as if they were indistinguishable. Time and again, teachers and examiners come across sentences such as 'In the novel *Romeo and Juliet...*' Though sometimes this can be just a slip of the pen, often this error is a good indicator of a weak response. Stronger responses fully appreciate the fact that *Romeo and Juliet* is a play, written for the stage, by a playwright and realise the implications of the writer's choice of the dramatic form.

Characterisation

Imagine you're a novelist writing a scene introducing a major character. Sit back and contemplate the rich variety of means at your disposal: You could begin with a quick pen portrait of their appearance, or you could have your characters say or do something significant. Alternatively, you could use your narrator to provide comments about, and background on, the character. Then again, you might take us into the character's thoughts and reveal what's going on inside their head. If you're trying to convey thought as it happens you could even use a stream of consciousness.

Now imagine that you're a playwright. Survey the far more limited means at your disposal. Though you could describe a character's appearance, you'd have to communicate this through stage directions, which, of course, a theatre audience would not be able to read or hear. The same holds true for background information and narratorial style comments about the character. And unless you're going to use the dramatic devices known as the aside and the soliloquy, as famously Shakespeare did in his great tragedies, you'll struggle to find a direct way to show what your character's really thinking.

As a playwright, action and dialogue, however, are your meat and drink. For a novelist being able to write dialogue is a useful skill; for a dramatist it's essential.

In general, drama focuses the audience's attention on a character's outward behaviour. Skillfully done, this can, of course, also reveal interior thoughts. Nevertheless, novels more easily give access to the workings of a character's mind. You may have noticed this when novels are adapted into films and directors have to make the decision about whether to use a voiceover to convey the narrator or characters' thoughts. Rarely does this work uncheesily well.

Settings

With a swish of his or her pen or run of fingers over a keyboard, a novelist can move quickly and painlessly from one setting to another. One chapter of a novel could be set in medieval Wells, the next on a distant planet in the distant future. The only limitation is the novelist's skill in rendering these worlds. What is true for geographical settings is also true for temporal ones. A novelist can write 'One hundred years later...' or track a character from cradle to grave or manipulate narrative time, using flashbacks and flashforwards.

Though a little more restricted, a modern film director can also move fairly easily between geographical and temporal settings and can cross-cut between them. Not so a playwright. Why? Because plays are written for an actual physical stage and radically changing a stage set during the action of a play is a tricky and potentially cumbersome business. Imagine your Medieval Wells hamlet, with its ramshackle thatched huts, pig pens and dirty streets. How are you going to transform this set to the dizzyingly futuristic world of Planet Zog in 2188 A.D.?

Possibly you could get your stage technicians to dismantle and construct the different stage sets while the audience waits patiently for the action to restart. But wouldn't that be clumsy, and rather break the spell you'd hope your play was weaving? More likely you'd use a break, perhaps between scenes or, better, during the interval for the major re-arrangement of stage scenery.

Practically speaking, how many different stage sets could you create for a single play? Minimalistic stage designs might allow you to employ more settings, but you'd still be far more restricted than a film director or a novelist. And then there's the cost. Theatres aren't usually loaded with money and elaborate stage sets are likely to be expensive. Another way out of this would be to have a pretty much bare and unchanging stage set and convey changes in scenes through the dialogue, a technique we'll see Shakespeare employ:

Character 1: What is this strange, futuristic place?
Character 2: Why, this must be the capital city of the Planet Zog
Character 1: And what would the correct date be now?

Etc.

Though, as we'll also see, Shakespeare tends to smuggle in this sort of exposition a little more subtly than we have.

Plays also tend to be written chronologically, i.e. with time always moving forward. Partly this is because as we watch plays in real time, it's difficult to convey to an audience that a particular scene is actually a flashback and is set in the past. There are exceptions, of course, to chronological trend. Notably Harold Pinter's *Betrayal*, for instance, in which the action of the play unfolds backwards from the present to past.

The time frame of a play also tends to be limited – days, weeks, perhaps even months, but very rarely years, decades or centuries. After all, it's not easy for an actor, or series of actors, to convincingly present characters aging over a prolonged period.

The stage and the page
Novelists and playwrights also have many things in common, but they work in distinctly different fields. You wouldn't want a chemist teaching you physics,

ideally, or depend on a rugby player to score a crucial FA cup goal. Nor would you want a vet to operate on you if you were ill, or for your GP to treat your poorly pet. And, with only a few exceptions, nor would you want to read a novel written by a playwright or witness a play written by a novelist. Precious few writers excel in both literary forms [Samuel Beckett, Chekhov and Michael Frayn come to mind, but few others] which underlines the point about the different demands of writing for the stage and for the page.

Novels take place in the theatre of the reader's mind; plays take place in an actual physical space, on an actual stage in real time. For the latter to happen a whole load of other people other than the writer have to be involved – directors, actors, designers, producers, technicians and so forth. And this takes us to the heart of another crucial difference between reading a play, reading a novel and seeing a play performed on a stage.

When we're reading a novel, the novelist can fill in the details of what is happening around the dialogue, such as gestures made by the characters:

'Did they even have pig-pens in medieval Wells?' asked Mikey, cocking his left eyebrow in a typically quizzical manner.

When we **read** a play, sometimes these details are apparent from stage directions. However, we cannot see what characters are doing while other characters are speaking and we can easily forget that silent characters are even present in a scene. When we **watch** a play, however, actors reveal how their characters are reacting to what each other are saying, and often these reactions convey crucial information about relationships, feelings and atmosphere. We know, for instance, how Tybalt reacts to Romeo's presence at the Capulet ball. But how are the other characters around him reacting?

Without the visual dimension of a performance it is all too easy for readers to ignore the things that are supposed to be happening in the narrative background while each character is speaking. If a play on a page is similar to a musical score, awaiting performance, a play on the stage is like the concert itself.

Focusing on the dramatic devices used by a playwright has a double benefit: Firstly, all good analytical literary essays concentrate on the writer's craft; secondly, such a focus emphasises to the examiner that you understand the nature of the type of text you're exploring, a play, and distinguishes you from many other readers who don't really appreciate this fact. In the next section we'll sharpen our focus on the playwright's technique by honing in on stagecraft.

Stagecraft

When writing about a novel, it's always productive to focus on narration. Narration includes narrative perspective, such as first and third person, types of narrator, such as naïve and unreliable, as well as narrative techniques, such as the use of dialogue, cross-cuts and flashbacks. Narration is worth focusing your attention on because it's an integral feature of all novels and short stories. In plays the equivalent of narration is stagecraft. Examining stagecraft is an incisive and revealing way to spot the writer at work. Some playwrights are able to use all the craft and resources of the theatre, namely set, props, costumes, lighting and music, while for various reasons [technical, artistic, budgetary] other playwrights may be more restricted.

Shakespeare, for instance, doesn't really use lighting in his plays, except notably in *The Winter's Tale*, because most of his plays were performed at the Globe theatre and in daylight. References to light, dark, the sun and the sky abound, however, in *Romeo and Juliet*, of course and a modern theatre director might wish to use a lighting rig to dim and brighten or add coloured filters to the light falling on the stage in order to indicate the time of day or night. Such is the power of Shakespeare's writing, however, that modern technology isn't needed. Shakespeare is able to conjure a sense of day or night via his use of words, as well as the occasional prop, such as a torch. His instructions on costume are also very limited, usually embedded within the texts, rather than stated separately in stage directions. Think, for example, of Malvolio's yellow cross-gartered stockings from *Twelfth Night*, Hamlet's inky suit of woe or whatever strange get-up Juliet's nurse has on that prompts calling her a 'sail'. On the other hand, the importance of costumes is underlined repeatedly in Shakespeare's plays by characters who disguise themselves by changing their clothes. For instance, Viola becoming Cesario in *Twelfth Night* or Kent and Edmund disguising themselves in *King Lear*. Repeatedly too, villainy in Shakespeare's plays tries to remain hidden under a layer of fine clothes. As Lady Macbeth instructs her husband, 'look like the innocent flower/ But be the serpent under't'.

The general sparsity of information about costumes has, however, allowed directors over the years to relocate Shakespeare's plays to all sorts of settings with a huge variety of matching costumes. In a recent RSC production of *Antony and Cleopatra*, for instance, the designs for the Egyptian queen's costumes were inspired by powerful contemporary female celebrities such as Beyoncé.

When a playwright is restricted in the range of stagecraft he or she can utilise, not only do the devices they employ become more prominent, but other integral aspects of stage business also become more significant. In *Romeo and Juliet*, for instance, exits and entrances are particularly important. Indeed the managing of exits and entrances is at the core of all plays. Exits facilitate changes in costume and allow actors to recover from or prepare for major scenes. Tracking these seemingly minor details always uncovers interesting and significant patterns, particularly in terms of which characters know what information at crucial points in the action.

Stage sets

As we mentioned in our discussion of the key differences between novels and plays, the latter invariably have fewer settings due to the fact that dramatic texts have to be physically realised in stage designs. And, as we also noted, changing from one elaborate stage set to another presents problems for directors and, potentially, for the finances of a production. What sort of choices does a stage designer have to make when creating a set? Firstly, a lot depends on the nature of the play, as well as the playwright, the director and the budget. Some playwrights are very particular about the settings of their plays and describe them in tremendous detail. Other playwrights leave these sorts of decisions to professional stage designers.

The American playwright Tennessee Williams wrote particularly poetic stage directions, such as those that open his play *A Streetcar Named Desire*: 'First dark of an evening in May' and the 'sky is a peculiarly tender blue, almost turquoise, which invests the scene with a kind of lyricism and gracefully attenuates the atmosphere of decay'. If that isn't enough to get a stage designer to shake and scratch their head, Williams finishes with a synesthetic poetic flourish 'you can almost feel the warm breath of the brown river' that is even more challenging to make tangible on a stage.

Other playwrights sketch out far more minimalistic sets. Samuel Beckett in *Waiting for Godot*, for instance, describes the stage set in the sparest way possible, using just six simple words: 'A country road. A tree. Evening'. [Despite the skeletal detail, in production, Beckett was notoriously specific and exacting about how he wanted the stage to be arranged.]

Even if the playwright doesn't provide a great deal of information about the precise setting, a director is likely to have an overall concept for a play and insist, albeit to varying degrees, that the set design fit with this. If, for instance, a director wishes to bring out the contemporary political resonances of a play such as *Julius Caesar* she or he might dress the characters like well-known American politicians and set the play in a place looking suspiciously like the modern White House. Similarly, Shakespeare's *Richard III* has often been relocated to an imagined modern fascistic state.

Given free reign, a stage designer has to decide how realistic, fantastical, symbolic and/or expressionist their stage set will be. The attempt to represent what looks like the real world on stage, as if the audience are looking in through an invisible fourth wall, is called verisimilitude and is the equivalent of photographic realism in fine art.

Stage sets for *Romeo and Juliet*

So what locations have we got to work with in this play? There are two different Italian cities, Verona and Mantua, several public spaces, the grand 'mansion' of the Capulets, with its various different rooms, including the 'great hall' and Juliet's bedroom with its famous balcony, an orchard, Friar Lawrence's cell, the churchyard and the gloomy tomb of the Capulets.

In productions on the Globe Stage a few judiciously placed props and/ or pieces of stage set have to suffice to conjure each of these very different public and private spaces, such as a bed for Juliet's room, perhaps. The balcony would not be a problem, as the Globe already has one and, by convention, the trapdoor leading down from the stage symbolises spaces under the ground, such as graves, tombs and even hell. An orchard might present more of a challenge. Rather than go for some sort of verisimilitude, directors tend to try to evoke the different atmosphere's associated with each setting. The lawlessness, boisterousness and sense of threat of the city streets, for example, compared to the quiet intimacy of Juliet's private bedroom. And this atmosphere can be generated more through the dialogue, how the actors read this and through their body language on stage.

Other stage directions

Most playwrights include stage directions within their scripts. By convention written in italics, these directions often establish the setting of a scene, outline lighting or music, convey physical action and sometimes also indicate to the actors how lines should be spoken. In *Who's Afraid of Virginia Woolf*, for example, the playwright, Edward Albee provides lots of extra information alongside the actual words his characters say. Here's a short extract that illustrates the point [in the extract a married woman, Martha, is flirting outrageously with a younger married man, Nick, in front of both his wife, Honey and Martha's own husband, George]:

MARTHA	[*to George...still staring at Nick, though*]: SHUT UP! [*Now, back to Nick*] Well, have you? Have you kept your body?
NICK	[*unselfconscious... almost encouraging her*]: It's still pretty good. I work out.
MARTHA	[*with a half-smile*]: Do you!
NICK	Yeah.
HONEY	Oh, yes...he has a very...firm body.
MARTHA	[*still with that smile... a private communication with Nick*] Have you! Oh, I think that's very nice.

Through the stage directions, Albee indicates to the actors where characters are looking, who they are at addressing at different moments, the tone they should adopt and even the facial expression the actors should put on. In addition, he uses capital letters as well as punctuation to convey tone and volume.

In contrast, Shakespeare's stage directions are usually minimalistic. As we've noted, at the start of scenes he establishes the setting with a just a few bold strokes of his quill. Take the opening scene's stage directions:

'Enter Sampson and Gregory, with swords and bucklers'.

There's very little sense of place, of a specific setting here. All that matters is that it's a public, street scene - neither the territory of the Capulet's nor the Montague's. Though lacking particularity, the public nature of the setting is important; it indicates how the feud between the two families can spill out and spread into the streets, disturbing the wider social order of Verona.

There are, however, subtler examples of stage directions in Shakespeare's plays, ones that are embedded within the dialogue. A few examples will illustrate the point. Often these directions suggest how the actors should play a particular moment. [Commonly in comedies written for and about the theatre, humour is generated by actors missing these sorts of prompts or responding to them too late. 'Is that the doorbell?' followed belatedly by the sound effect of a doorbell ringing is a classic example.]

In the opening scene, Gregory instructs Sampson to 'draw' his 'tool' and in the following line Sampson says that his 'naked weapon is out'. Clearly this line won't make much sense if the actor hasn't already drawn his sword. Similarly the stage direction for the actors to insult each other through a rude gesture, biting their thumbs, is embedded within their speech. In the last scene of the play, no stage direction tells the actor playing Juliet to drink the poison, whereas there is one about stabbing herself with the dagger. Juliet's words, however, make it clear that she does desperately pick up the cup and drink from it.

A critic once commented that, unlike a modern film or even theatre director, Shakespeare didn't have any spectacular special effects at this disposal. But rather than detracting from his plays, this limitation is partly responsible for what makes them so extraordinary. Because for Shakespeare his language has to deliver these special effects. And often the way Shakespeare's language is crafted indicates to an actor how to play a line or even a speech, as well as the atmosphere the director should seek to evoke on stage.

Entrances and exits

Paying close attention to who is and who isn't present in a scene, who comes in and who goes out, is always rewarding. Sometimes, indeed, the significance of a character's silent presence can be made more explicit on a stage than it might appear on the page and, equally, a character's absence from a scene may also be highly significant. The arrival of characters too late in a scene or their premature exit from one so that they miss crucial information are also worth noting, especially in this play, where these sorts of near misses occur frequently, often with devastating impact.

Props

Props can, of course, be used in all manner of ways. In Arthur Miller's *The Crucible* at the climax of the play the protagonist, John Proctor signs a false confession of having committed witchcraft on a piece of paper. But when he is asked to give up this parchment by the court officials he will not, and his final defiance is shown dramatically when he tears this prop in half. In

Shakespeare's tragedy *King Lear*, the physical ring of the crown is an emblem of the impossibility of splitting the kingdom successfully between Lear's daughters and therefore of the foolishness of the king's plan. In *Hamlet* the iconic image of Prince Hamlet holding in his hand dead Yorick's skull emblematises the play's theme of mortality. In many of Shakespeare's plays props in the form of physical letters are intercepted and fall dangerously into the wrong hands, moving on the plot. In the case of *Romeo and Juliet*, Benvolio and Romeo's interception of Capulet's invite to his party is, of course, crucial to the plot.

Props can also be used as metonyms, signals of character - heroes in Shakespeare's plays invariably carry and brandish swords, not daggers, while foppish characters carry nosegays and villains carry bottles of poison. Props can be used to heighten a dramatic effect and, as in the example from *The Crucible*, to tell in a single image or action something it would take words longer to do.

Before you read the next section list any props you can remember appearing in the play. Try to arrange them in chronological order. Then write next to each one how they are used by the dramatist. The props in the play include a ring, keys, flowers, purses, crow-bars, spades, torches, lanterns and a mattock. The most important of these props are the deadly ones – the weapons, various bottles of potion and more indirectly, fatal letters.

Weapons

Unsurprisingly, in a play bristling with so much violence, there are lots of references to swords and to dangerous weapons of various types and sizes. From Act I, Scene 1 onwards swords feature particularly heavily, physically brandished on stage and also mentioned frequently in the dialogue. Not only the aristocratic characters, but also the humble serving men, Sampson, Gregory and Abram carry swords, suggesting the ubiquity of deadly weapons in their culture. The carrying of such dangerous weapons, particularly by young men, means that petty quarrels can quickly flare-up into something far more serious, even, as we shall witness, fatal. But it is not just the hot-headed young men who cause this violence. Seeing the affray, Lord Capulet calls for his 'long sword' and when Lord Montague arrives on the scene he 'flourishes his blade' at his enemy. If the young are recklessly violent, they have learnt this behaviour from their elders and supposed betters.

But, that's not quite precise enough. Because it's not just the young nor indeed specifically both the old and the young who carry these weapons. It's  specifically male characters, some of whom are young men, not much more than boys. The ubiquity and fetishization of swords in the play resonates, of course, with modern concerns about knife crime and gun culture. The intimate connection between swords, the almost-sport of 'sword play', violence and male identity in *Romeo and Juliet* is signalled in the first scene through provocative boasts of thrusting an enemy's 'maids to the wall' and most obviously via Sampson's warning that his 'naked weapon is out'. In short, swords are phallic symbols, symbols of specifically masculine power.

When the 'officers of the Watch' enter the scene they carry 'clubs and partisans' [long, speared poles]. These weapons are less associated with noble characters in Shakespeare's plays, but are just as effective in a more rudimentary way.

Generally daggers, like poison, in Shakespeare's plays are either associated with villains or with terrible acts and crimes. Think of the phrase 'cloak and dagger'. You might recall that in *Macbeth* Donalbain warns his brother that where they are there are 'daggers in men's smiles' and that the assassins who kill Banquo and the Macduff family carry daggers, not swords. Moreover, it is a dagger Macbeth sees hovering supernaturally before him as he crosses his castle at night in order to murder King Duncan. And, of course, Macbeth does use daggers to assassinate the king, the weapons also used by the assassins in *Julius Caesar*.

At various points in the play [excuse the pun] both Romeo and Juliet have daggers on their person or keep them close by. When Romeo visits Friar

Lawrence [Act III, Scene 3] in despair he 'offers to stab himself' but the [rather impressively] the Nurse 'snatches the dagger away'. Similarly in Act IV, Scene

3 Juliet keeps a dagger by her bed in case the potion doesn't work and she wakes the following morning to be married to Parris. Daggers, then, are associated with self-destruction in a way that swords are not. And, of course, at the end of the play, Juliet kills herself with Romeo's dagger.

In Elizabethan society suicide was one of the most heinous of crimes, a sin against God that many believed doomed the victims soul to hell. Hence it is entirely fitting that a weapon associated with evil acts is used in the play. On the other hand, however, Elizabethan culture [and Shakespeare's plays] was influenced by classical literature and in Roman society committing suicide could be a noble way of avoiding shame and dishonour. The use of this villainous prop, the dagger, we might conclude, is emblematic of the complex and nuanced way in which the two heroic lovers are presented in the play.

Bottles of potion

Generally in Shakespeare's work, poison is associated with Machiavellian villains. In *Hamlet* Claudius poisons his brother to seize the throne. In *King Lear*, Goneril poisons her sister, Regan. More metaphorically, Iago in *Othello* poisons the protagonist's mind with insinuations about his wife. Machiavellian villains are sneaky and underhand; they connive, trick and plot to destroy their enemies and commit murder in seemingly undetectable ways. When Juliet hesitates before drinking from the 'vial' in Act IV, Scene 3, she fears that Father

Lawrence may have become a Machiavel in order to cover up his role in her marriage:

What if it be poison which the Friar
Subtly hath ministered to have me dead
Lest in this marriage he should be dishonoured,
Because he married me before to Romeo?

It's not an unreasonable fear, is it? It is possible that the Friar is a character who appears good and moral on the surface, but is, or perhaps becomes, driven by selfish motives. He would potentially face severe punishment if his role in the marriage is discovered, so he does have a motive for getting rid of the evidence.

However, Juliet is right to dismiss this fear and in just one line. The Friar is a 'holy man' and from what the audience have witnessed of him in the play so far there is no indication that he has been secretly plotting against the lovers and he has no overall motivation to work against them. The brief doubt about the Friar combines with other perfectly reasonable fears Juliet has about drinking the potion. These fears – that the timing will be wrong, the terror of the grave and so forth – heighten the dramatic tension and convey Juliet's great courage. As Juliet finally drinks dramatically from the vial everyone in the audience must be wondering whether we could find so much courage, trust and faith if we were in her shoes.

As with the daggers, like Juliet, Romeo also has a bottle of potion to drink, but, unlike her, he knows his is almost certainly poison. [His purchase of the bottle is discussed in our essay on Romeo where we argue his actions do not reflect favourably on his character.] Also like Juliet, Romeo is given a soliloquy in the run-up to his drinking the cup of poison. And once again, Shakespeare ratchets up the dramatic tension before Romeo's final fatal act.

As with the daggers, there is some moral ambiguity about Romeo's self-slaughter. Even more than daggers, poison is associated in Shakespeare's plays with villains. Perhaps drinking poison requires a little less courage than stabbing oneself with a dagger and an Elizabethan audience is likely to have been more unsympathetic to Romeo's action that a modern audience might be. Another layer of ambiguity is added by the connection of potions in the play with medicinal properties as well as with fatal ones. For example, Mercutio imagined Romeo had been drugged by love. Moreover, there are two apothecaries in the play, one who will sell poison, the other a holy Friar. And in his soliloquy in Act II, Scene 3 Friar Lawrence describes how within the 'infant rind' of one 'weak flower' 'poison has residence' but also 'medicine power'.

Intercepted letters

A character stands on stage, silently reading a letter full of vital, urgent news and often important plot exposition. Leaning in, or over their shoulder, other characters crowd close, with baited-breath, trying to discover the truth. This eager audience on stage mirrors the audience in the auditorium, who also have to wait on tenterhooks for the revelation of the letter's content. Perhaps the letter has been intercepted and has fallen into the wrong hands and will inadvertently uncover secret plots and dire machinations. It's a very effective dramatic device and one frequently exploited by Shakespeare. In fact letters fly around throughout Shakespeare's plays, being written, dispatched, intercepted and read by a host of eager characters. The Machiavellian Edmund in *King Lear* forges a letter exposing his brother's apparent plot against their father's life. [His brother is innocent and unawares]. In the same

play, the King's daughter, Goneril, sends a fatal letter via her loyal servant who is killed before he can deliver it to its intended recipient. Macbeth writes home to his wife to tell her about his strange meeting with the witches. Captured by pirates after leaving Elsinore, Hamlet sends his friend Horatio a letter which helpfully updates the audience about what he has been doing while off-stage. Hamlet also intercepts the secret letter written by his uncle Claudius ordering the English king to murder Hamlet and, with a little editing of the letter, the Prince ensures that the letter seals the fate of characters who have betrayed him. Malvolio in *Twelfth Night* finds a love letter he believes to be written by his mistress, with disastrous comic consequences. And so on. Shakespeare loved using letters, often letters gone astray, in his plays.

Letters are so important because they seem to confirm things in black and white. They are hard, indisputable proof. Or seem to be: Edmund's father, the Duke of Gloucester, would never have believed that his other son, Edgar, was plotting to murder him if he had not thought he'd read it for himself in a letter he didn't know was forged. It is unlikely the conspiring servants could have persuaded Malvolio's of his mistress' affections without the ruse of the letter. It is fortunate in Shakespeare's plays that so many characters are adept at forging each other's handwriting.

Of course, there are two crucial letters in *Romeo and Juliet*. The first is Capulet's invite to his masked ball intercepted by Romeo and his friends. Were it not for the illiteracy of Capulet's servant, the whole narrative of the play could not have taken place. That's a lot of weight on one letter. The other letter is Friar Lawrence's to Romeo. The letter that would explain the plan for Juliet to drink the sleeping potion. The letter that would have ensured Romeo knew that Juliet was not really dead. The letter that would have saved both their lives. The letter that, fatally and fatefully, never arrived. On the non-delivery of that letter hangs the weight of both their deaths.

Costumes

In Shakespeare's time the sumptuary laws were still in place. These laws dictated what people could and could not wear depending on their status in society. Fundamentally, the higher your status the greater the range of clothes and material you were allowed to wear. Clearly in Shakespeare's plays the power of royal characters can be emphasized on stage by the richness of the costumes chosen for them.

In some of his plays Shakespeare specifies exactly how particular characters should be dressed. In *King Lear*, Edgar as Mad Tom, for instance, is dressed in nothing but rags, Lear enters at one point with a crown of flowers on his head and stage directions informs us that on her return to England Lear's exiled daughter, Cordelia, is wearing armour. Famously in *Hamlet* the titular character dresses predominantly in black to express his continued mourning for his dead father. In *Twelfth Night* Shakespeare is very precise about Malvolio's comical attire when he goes to court his mistress, Olivia.

Although Shakespeare isn't specific about the costumes of the Capulets and Montagues, many productions have emphasised the gang-like quality of each family and their followers by dressing members of the same family in similar outfits or colours. In Baz Luhrmann's 1996 film of the play, for instance, the Montagues are dressed like beach bums, with bright floral shirts and shorts, while the Capulets are slick in black and red leather. Notably, in this film version, neither Romeo or Juliet follow their family's dress code. Similarly, in the musical loosely based on the play, *West Side Story* the two families are replaced by two gangs, the sharks and the jets, with the former dressed in bright, vivid colours and the latter in more muted colours and tones.

Perhaps the most crucial pieces of costume in the whole play are the masks worn at the masked ball. These masks allow the Montagues to mix almost undetected by the Capulets, so without them the two lovers could not have met. In addition, the masks make literal and physically tangible a central running theme in the play, the way in which characters play various roles like actors and, at times, have to pretend to be things they are not.

Lighting

In modern theatres lighting can be used starkly and boldly, such as in picking out a main character in a bright spotlight, or it can be used more subtly to convey mood and generate atmosphere. Intense white light makes everything on stage look stark and exposed; blue lights help to create a sense of coolness, whereas yellows, oranges and reds generate a sense of warmth and even passion. Floor lights can light an actor from beneath, making them look powerful and threatening. Light coming down on them from above can cause an actor to look vulnerable and threatened, or even angelic. Changes of lighting between scenes are common ways of changing the pervasive atmosphere.

However, for most of his theatrical career, Shakespeare was writing for the Globe theatre where performances took place only during daylight hours. Only when his plays were performed at the indoor theatre at Blackfriars, from around 1608 could Shakespeare employ lighting effects. Before that Shakespeare had to conjure a sense of light and, especially, darkness through the power of his verse, making the audience imagine things they couldn't actually see.

There are many references to lighting in the play, indicating where scenes are played in daylight or night-time. The torches at the masked ball, for instance, indicate that the scene takes place in darkness - suitable lighting for the excitement and mystery of the ball. The same prop, the 'torch' reappears, of course, at the end of the play when Paris and Romeo enter the Capulet vault. Here the prop amplifies the dramatic irony – the audience knows Juliet is already dead and can see clearly – while the characters stumble around in darkness that is both literal and metaphoric.

Light and darkness are also symbolic in other ways too. Frequent references to day and night in the play and the one becoming the other operate within a wider structural pattern of opposites. The references also contribute to the feeling throughout that everything is going too fast, time is short, running out, that the lovers never have quite enough time or light.

The nature of the play

What is a tragedy?

According to *The Complete A-Z English Literature Handbook* a tragedy is a 'drama which ends disastrously' and falls into two broad types:

- Greek tragedy, where fate brings about the downfall of the character[s].
- Shakespearean tragedy, where a character has free will and their fatal flaw causes the downfall.

As you shall discover when you read our essays on the tragic protagonists of *Romeo and Juliet* the second half of that second point is much disputed by literary academics and Shakespeare scholars. And, in fact, it seems that the description above of a Greek tragedy fits *Romeo and Juliet* rather snugly.

According to Jennifer Wallace in *The Cambridge Introduction to Tragedy*, 'Tragedy is an art form created to confront the most difficult experiences we face; death, loss, injustice, thwarted passion, despair.' Wallace goes on to explain that 'questions about the causes of suffering, which are raised in each culture, are posed powerfully in tragedy.'[1] That's helpful, but couldn't we say the same sorts of things about the academic subject of philosophy?

---

[1] *The Cambridge Introduction to Tragedy.*

While, on the one hand, there are critics, such as Terry Eagleton, who argue the only thing that the plays we call tragedies have in common is that they are 'very, very sad', on the other hand, many other critics argue that all literary tragedies share distinctive common formal features which separate them from real-life stories of great unhappiness. And, if we shrink our perspective down from tragedies as a whole art form to just Shakespeare's versions, we'll discover there's not much academic agreement either about what attributes Shakespeare's plays have in common:

'An eminent Shakespearian scholar famously remarked that there is no such thing as Shakespearian Tragedy; there are only Shakespearian tragedies'.

So begins Tom McAlindon's essay *What is a Shakespearian Tragedy?*[2] The author goes on to point out how attempts to define tragedy, such as those we've quoted above, tend to 'give a static impression of the genre and incline towards prescriptivism', ignoring the fact that literary genres constantly change and develop over time.

So, to sum up: The definition of 'tragedy' is hotly contested. So too is the definition of Shakespearian Tragedy. Indeed, more fundamentally, even the idea of defining both these terms is itself contested within literary criticism. So where does that leave us with *Romeo and Juliet*? Perhaps a sensible way to try to find a route out of the academic fogginess is to start at the beginning and then navigate our way from that fixed point. In terms of defining tragedy as an art form, Aristotle's theories of tragedy make a good starting point.

Aristotle

Often it is assumed that Aristotle was setting down a prescriptivist rule book for writing tragedies, a kind of classical instruction manual for aspiring playwrights to follow. This assumption is mistaken. In fact, Aristotle, in his

---

[2] *The Cambridge Companion to Tragedy,*

Poetics, was describing the features of classical tragedies as he saw them. Taken as prescriptivist or descriptivist, what is certain is that Aristotle's ideas about tragedies have been hugely influential. In particular, four key ideas have helped shape the ways tragedies have been written and read for hundreds of years. These ideas concern:

i.   the nature of the protagonist
ii.   the cause of tragic action
iii. the significance of plot
iv.   the emotional effect of tragedy on an audience.

For our purposes, the first two of these concepts are particularly interesting.

The protagonist in classical tragedy is always high-born, a prince or king or someone of equivalent social status. This means their fall is as precipitous and dramatic as possible - right from the top to the very bottom of society - in a way that the fall of someone from the bottom to the bottom of society would not be. As the tragic hero or heroine is high-born and they fall along way, the impact sends shockwaves out across the whole world of the play, creating cracks and fissures in the social fabric. Crucially, the primary cause of the fall is a fault in the tragic protagonist. Historically Shakespearian critics often conceived of the tragic flaw, or hamartia, in psychological terms, but according to Aristotle it could equally be a terrible decision made by the tragic hero.

Read through an Aristotelian critical perspective, *Romeo and Juliet* is a play fundamentally about its protagonists, whose tragic fall is precipitated by their hamartia. Different critics might argue about what this hamartia might be and whether both Romeo and Juliet have the same fatal flaw.

Modern criticism

However, most modern Shakespearian critics argue that an Aristotelian approach to tragedy over-emphasises the importance of the tragic hero and of characters in general. These critics are more interested in the role of society and of history in shaping the experience of characters. Read through this kind of framework, the tragedy stems from irresolvable, conflicting forces within the period in which Shakespeare was writing, a period that historians call the early modern. So, for instance, a modern critic might argue that *Romeo and Juliet* dramatises a conflict between traditional, essential feudal values – of loyalty, duty to your parents, honour and so forth – and a new Renaissance spirit of individualism and self-determination.

In addition, though it was listed as such in the First Folio, we might ask whether *Romeo and Juliet* really fits the genre of tragedy. For much of the play, it seems more like a comedy: the focus is on family rather than the affairs of the state; the principal characters fall in love and face significant obstacles to fulfilling this love. But comedies are defined by their endings; in comedies the lovers eventually overcome the obstacles and are married at the end of the play. And this is one of the reasons why the play is so heart breaking; a happy comic resolution is so desperately near at hand, but then is so decisively whipped away.

The big themes

Love

Romeo and Juliet is not a love story. This is a story about two teenagers with little or no experience of the world, who manage to find each other, get married, have sex, commit murder and then take their own lives, all in the space of three days and without anyone really noticing for most of the time. This isn't love. This is death, pride, anger and despair, and the lovers are just a vehicle for all the bottled-up hatred, the feuding and rancour, in the world of the play to spill out.

The play does, however, explore many of the *trappings* of love and, though brief, the embryonic romance propels us through a lifetime of emotion and experience in a very compressed, high octane narrative. We see: lust, attraction, obsession, impulsiveness, desire, anxiety, confusion, passion, anger, elation, grief, despair. This 'not-a-love-story' shows that love is, perhaps, not one single state of being, but a whole host of powerful emotions which are changeable. Love is abstract and elusive, and this play reflects many ideas about love which we see throughout the wider world of Shakespeare.

Love as a weakener

At the start of the play, Romeo is brought low by unrequited love. Though we might call it nothing more than boyish lust, his despair over Roseline makes him less than himself, 'tut, I have lost myself; I am not here.' Romeo has been substantially altered by this attachment. This is compounded later in the play; Romeo's marriage to Juliet apparently makes him 'effeminate' and 'soften[s] valour's steel.' Shakespearean men who develop deep attachments to women often allow themselves to be altered by those new loyalties and 'soft' emotions. In *Much Ado about Nothing*, Benedict swears, 'I will not be forsworn but love may transform me to an oyster.' [Act II, Scene 3] Shakespeare sets up an opposition between strength and manliness on one side, and the state of love and weakness on the other, as if mere proximity to women reduces a man's power.

Love as a driver

Love is instant in many of Shakespeare's plays, 'who ever loved that loved not at first sight?' [As You Like It, Act III, Scene 5] In *Romeo and Juliet,* from the moment the initial attraction takes hold, the narrative races through a series of dramatic events. Love, therefore, is a driver for plot. Shakespeare uses passionate love as an emotive pull for the audience and to enhance the tragedy of the lovers' final moments. Their love is a particular kind of youthful infatuation akin to mania; Romeo in particular appears overtaken by the kind of intense, primal emotion which the Greeks called 'Eros' - romantic, passionate love. His first encounter with Juliet prompts heavenly visions and grandiose comparisons between her eyes and those of the stars. This young love is a sort of mania; it becomes the force which pulls the lovers inexorably to their deaths.

Love in contrast - 'death-marked love'

From the outset of this play, Shakespeare pairs love with death, love with hate, love with pain. There is never a moment that death or violence are absent from the stage and this, paired with the joyous exuberance of love, produces constant tension. For example, the opening of the play is a violent scene in the street laced with threats of sexual violence, 'the heads of their maidens,' and the introduction of Tybalt, the consummate villain who 'hate[s]' peace. His unreasonable, mindless antagonism provides the backdrop for an equally passionate romantic encounter just a few scenes later. Love and hate exist in tandem throughout the drama.

Shakespeare and love

Shakespeare's sonnets show us that the greatest love is deep, profound and enduring. It is 'an ever-fixed mark' that even in a 'tempest' is 'never shaken'. In stark contrast, Romeo and Juliet experience the kind of brief, passionate love which dies 'like fire and powder.' It is tempting to suggest that Shakespeare is critical of this kind of quickfire emotion - that he is portraying the foolishness of the young who do not truly understand lasting love. It might be more helpful, though, to see this play as an acknowledgement that there are many iterations of love at every stage of life, and that these emotions dictate human behaviour. This play challenges our ideas of what we expect from parental love, and shows us the damage which that parent-child bond can do. It depicts the powerful love between friends which leads to Romeo's maddening grief and the murder of Tybalt. And finally, Shakespeare portrays the profound exhilaration of young romantic love and its destructive potential. Love conquers reason and dictates human action.

Freedom

Shakespeare is fascinated by freedom. In his comedies, characters find new possibilities and license in mystical worlds; in *As You Like It*, Rosalind gains liberty in the Forest of Arden; in *Twelfth Night*, Viola gains freedoms as a boy which she would never have otherwise had as a woman alone in a strange place. Freedom is clearly something which men had and women did not. Many of Shakespeare's women begin his plays as obedient daughters who are under pressure from societal expectations, and the ensuing drama often

follows their journey to subvert those pressures and resolve conflict in one way or another. In the tragedies, these restrictions and controlling forces often end in the death of those women who dare to break from their socially approved path. Juliet is one of a line of Shakespeare's tragic heroines who pay for their transgressions with their lives.

Societal ideas of what women should be were not just theoretical, they were enacted physically. During the 16th Century, women who had the audacity to speak against men were labelled as 'scolds' and often subjected to cruel and humiliating practices: water torture through the 'cucking stool'; forced wearing of the 'scold's bridle'. Each of these practices was accompanied by communal shaming and a parade through the town. Boose describes them as 'a carnival experience, one that literally placed women at the center of a mocking parade'.[3] The legal crime of being a 'scold' was not actually removed from English and Welsh law until 1967. *The Taming of the Shrew* depicts such a woman being tamed 'from a wild Kate to a Kate/ conformable as other household Kates.' The freedom of women was seen by Shakespeare's contemporaries as a potential evil and disturbance of the peace. Lord Capulet's threat that he will 'drag' Juliet on a 'hurdle' to the church, and the assertion that she may 'hang, beg, starve, die in the streets,' does not seem so unusual in this context.

---

[3] Boose, E, Scolding *Brides and Bridling Scolds: Taming the Woman's Unruly Member*, Shakespeare Quarterly.

Juliet could never be described as a 'scold.' She is not a wild, wilful child. She begins the play as a dutiful daughter who will go only so far as her father's 'consent' will allow her. Like Shakespeare's other tragic heroines, her defiance appears to be a tool to highlight the flaws of the men around her. In *King Lear*, Cordelia's refusal to pander to her father exposes his hubris and folly at the start of the

play. In Juliet's case, her love for Romeo and subsequent actions serve to highlight the potentially destructive nature of the male ego. The feud and revenge killings are damaging to wider society and people's freedom to live a full, happy life: Juliet's vulnerability and eventual demise highlight this.

Freedom and entrapment are further explored by the use of birds and flight in this play. Romeo insists that love has given him 'light wings' to transcend 'stony limits' [Act II, Scene 2]. In some cases, Shakespeare seems to be arguing that love itself is a form of freedom. At the opening of the play, love-sick Romeo likens love to a 'burden' and a 'heavy weight,' but Mercutio instructs him to 'borrow Cupid's wings and soar with them above a common bond.' The suggestion here is that real love exists above the petty affairs of every day; lovers have the power to see and experience something more profound and lofty than the barriers and oppression which limit us. Perhaps the two lovers are the only characters in the play who have that gift of freedom from the feud; their love enables them to see beyond hate.

This flight imagery is developed by frequent reference to birds,

> I would have thee gone.
> And yet no further than a wanton's bird,
> That lets it hop a little from his hand
> Like a poor prisoner in his twisted gyves,
> And with a silken thread *plucks it back again,*
> *So loving-jealous of his liberty.*

This statement is simultaneously loving and controlling. Juliet wishes that

Romeo could be brought back to her on a tether, as a child might pull back a pet bird on a string. The implication is that a bird has the potential for flight and 'liberty' - as a man, Romeo has far greater liberty than Juliet to go where he will, and Juliet wants to keep him close to her. This bird metaphor goes in the other direction, too. Romeo's first sight of Juliet prompts this description, 'so shows a snowy dove trooping with crows' [Act I, Scene 5]. Juliet, by this logic, is a symbol of peace amongst more sinister creatures. Crows are often associated with death and omens of dark futures. The dove, as the creature which assured Noah that the flood had receded and land was near, represents hope, faith and peace. In this scene, Juliet represents goodness and purity surrounded by danger and darkness. The powerful symbolism of birds is used by Shakespeare throughout this play to highlight the plight of the lovers as the sole positive element in the midst of a broken society. The physical fragility of birds, paired with their natural beauty, perhaps also implies that their fledgling relationship is vulnerable to these external pressures. The tragic ending of these two lovers is perhaps the inevitable consequence of applying power and control to something as delicate as love.

To love is a form of freedom. Hermia craves the freedom to love Lysander, but her life is threatened and it takes a magical intervention to make her dream a reality. Desdemona choses to freely love Othello across barriers of race and age, but this results in her death. Ophelia's love for Hamlet is rewarded with a watery grave. These women are defined by their desire for freedom - to choose who to love and how to live in a world controlled by men. Kottman argues that *Romeo and Juliet* 'exposes a conflict between the lovers' desires and the reigning demands of family, civic and social norms'[4]. I would go further than this and suggest that this play explores the very nature of love itself as a wild and unruly passion which goes against the fabric of a regimented society. Gender, class and religion in 16th Century England limited people's freedoms, and Shakespeare's plays often depict love as the only force pushing back against these barriers.

---

[4] Kottman, P, *Defying the Stars; Tragic Love as a Struggle for Freedom in Romeo and Juliet*, Shakespeare Quarterly,

Masculinity

Masculinity jumps off the stage from the first scene in *Romeo and Juliet* and acts as a powerful driver which propels the play to its bloody conclusion. If we define 'masculinity' during the Renaissance as being related to strength and  patriarchal power, it would be tempting to argue that this play presents a simple view: that an aggressive, toxic masculinity is the cause of human tragedy. However, this is an unhelpful generalisation. In this play, Shakespeare offers us a plethora of different male characters, all of whom give us different versions of what 'masculinity' might mean. Tybalt provides a two-dimensional 'angry' man who is a catalyst for physical violence, but characters such as the changeable Capulet and the pensive Mercutio provide nuance to the 'angry man' figure. The characters of Benvolio and Friar Lawrence are reasoned, calm and peaceable, and Romeo himself rolls all of these traits into one; he is aggressive and impulsive alongside being reasoned and conciliatory. Masculinity is far from simple.

In the opening scene, Sampson and Gregory revel their compulsion to fight. Gregory implies that Sampson is, 'not quick to strike,' and Sampson replies by saying, 'a dog of the house of Capulet moves me'. The suggestion here is that Sampson is always eager to fight, at any moment, given cause. Their discussion quickly develops and the two men goad each other into more extreme and disturbing oaths; Sampson states that he would 'cut of the heads of the maidens, or their maidenheads', suggesting that he would be prepared to murder or rape the Capulet women. This conversation may be brief, but it lays bare the nature of male power in this play and wider society. Generally larger and stronger than women and higher in social status, men could genuinely hold power over women and threaten their safety. These servants may be only minor characters but, when coupled with the threats made against Juliet's life by her own father later in the play, this conversation provides a very clear sense of the gulf between men and women. Any discussion of masculinity, then, must be partly about physical violence and its relation to power.

This theme of violence and the men who wield it is threaded throughout the entire play, even by those characters who truly do not wish to fight. Tybalt provides a fascinating opportunity for contrast with various other characters in the play. His own eagerness to fight is clear from his opening statements, 'peace, I hate the word,' so the audience is not shocked when he attempts to incite violence at the ball, or when he kills Mercutio. We are, however, shown a different side to masculinity in Lord Capulet. His refusal to be drawn into a fight in Act I, Scene 5 is because he understands his role as a host, 'you'll make a mutiny among my guests'. Capulet's masculine role in this scenario is as a generous and welcoming host; a pillar of the community. Masculinity, then, is not purely governed by violence. Similarly, Tybalt provides a stark contrast with Romeo in Act III, Scene 1, where he is the instigator of the tragic fight, but Romeo is resistant and seeks peace. Romeo is not thinking of defending his own honour in a duel, but in being a good husband to his new bride. He says to Tybalt, 'I love thee more than thou canst devise', trying, in vain, to avoid a brawl. Here we see yet another side to masculinity; upholding family bonds and taking seriously the role of a husband. By providing Tybalt as a caricature of the 'angry' man, Shakespeare allows us to see other masculine traits in sharper relief.

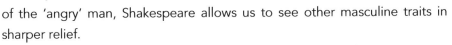

Some critics have argued that Romeo is Shakespeare's model of what the ideal man should be. He is a character who we can examine through a range of different attitudes across the play. He is love-sick, lustful and downcast in the opening of the play, and audience members are often quick to groan and call this immature teenage behaviour. Romeo's assertion that 'sad hours seem long' and his rather dramatic descriptions of love and emotion, 'feather of lead, bright smoke', could initially appear shallow and insincere. Shakespeare, however, grants Romeo moments of real maturity and clarity later in the play. If Romeo is lustful and insincere at the start, he has far more control over his actions later on. Aside from his reluctance to fight, he displays remarkable restraint on meeting Paris in Act V, Scene 3. Romeo's masculinity in this scene is not predicated on fighting a man who wanted to marry his wife. Instead he avoids that violent encounter in order to be with Juliet in the tomb. He does not want to fight, he wants to love and grieve. Romeo begs Paris to stand aside,

> I beseech thee, youth,
> Put not another sin upon my head,
> By urging me to fury: O, be gone!
> By heaven, I love thee better than myself.

Where Mercutio and Tybalt saw no eternal consequence to their violent, destructive actions, Romeo recognises that he has already committed sin and that he is in danger of being 'urg(ed)' to 'fury'. This is a man who knows himself and his aggressive nature, and is attempting to avoid tragedy. Where Tybalt would have waded in, Romeo does what he can to prevent Paris' death. In Romeo, Shakespeare gives us a man who is secure in his masculine identity; he is Juliet's husband, and that responsibility supersedes everything else.

This play explores masculinity, but does not offer a simple view of what it is to be male. Violence and aggression are entirely the domain of the male characters, but Shakespeare appears to present us with a sympathetic protagonist who actively seeks to avoid catastrophe by embracing another definition of masculinity. Romeo's status as a husband changes his approach to conflict and, though the play still ends in tragedy, Romeo's attempts to avoid violence are a powerful argument that there may be more strength in choosing the peaceful path.

Death and Fate

Shakespeare's tragedies follow a steady pattern: poor decisions and malevolent forces push flawed characters inexorably toward their own destruction. The title of 'tragedy' immediately informs an audience that there will be suffering and death for their viewing pleasure, and they expect to see the bounds of human pain and emotion being tested on stage. In many of Shakespeare's tragedies, the characters point to the stars; their destiny is foretold and inescapable. No tragedy is more explicitly driven by this belief than *Romeo and Juliet*, where the tragic story of the 'star-crossed lovers' is told in brief before the play even begins. The Prologue establishes a pre-destined path where the audience can never hope to see a 'happy ending'. Why, then, do audiences watch tragedy on stage? Adrian Poole says, 'Tragedy is a precious word. We use it to confer dignity and value on violence, catastrophe, agony and bereavement. *Tragedy* claims that *this* death is exceptional'. When we watch a Shakespeare tragedy, we witness death in a romanticised, heightened form. It is more poignant and moving because we are emotionally tied to a narrative arc and to sympathetic characters.

Death, put bluntly, is a form of fascinating entertainment in literature and the theatre, but Shakespeare's Renaissance audience might be accused of having an unhealthy morbid obsession. As Andrew Dickson puts it, 'mortality rates were high, especially for newborns and young children, and centuries before  the invention of vaccination threats such as bubonic plague, typhus, smallpox and cholera were deadly real. One in ten children died before their first birthday; not many people made it far beyond their sixtieth. Death and the rituals used to shape and cope with it were an everyday sight in a metropolis such as London: executions were enthusiastically attended, funerals were public and mourning rites were highly visible'.[5]

So death was a prominent part of people's everyday lives, and alongside that came beliefs in astrology and destiny which we see played out in *Romeo and*

---

[5] Dickson, 'I am Every Dead Thing: John Donne and Death', British Library Online.

Juliet.

The link between tragedy and fate goes back as far as Greek Tragedy, 'Fortune with constant ebb and flow, casts down and raises high alike the

prosperous and wretched' [Antigone]. A major difference between Greek and Shakespearean tragedy is that in Greek tragedy there are external factors at play. No matter how good or righteous the hero, they may still die or suffer because of the whim of a god. We only have to look at the plight of Hercules to see that he was simply a pawn in a much larger game. In Shakespeare's plays, however, the fate of characters seems determined partly by their own flaws; Lear's demise is initiated by his own ego and stubbornness, Macbeth's by his vaulting ambition and the Montagues and Capulets lose their children because of their feuding and hatred.

Throughout the play, we are constantly reminded of the fate of the lovers by repeated warnings, misgivings and visions. Before meeting Juliet, Romeo has a premonition, 'my mind misgives;/ Some consequence, yet hanging in the stars' [Act I, Scene 4]. This explicit reference to 'stars' brings us back to the 'star-crossed lovers' from the prologue and acts as a thread which takes us through to the bitter end. On hearing of Juliet's death in Act V, Scene 1, Romeo exclaims, 'I defy you, stars'. Romeo suggests in this moment that he will attempt to change the reality of her death, in the same breath as admitting that their fate is written in the 'stars', and thus inescapable.

Fate and the threat of death sits over the play like a storm cloud. We are never free from it, and this creates a constant tension which mars all the moments where we might otherwise have found temporary light relief. In Act III, Scene 5, where the lovers are married, together and harmonious, Juliet has a vision,

> I have an ill-divining soul.
> Methinks I see thee now, thou art so low
> As one dead in the bottom of a tomb.

At this supposedly happy moment of marital bliss, Juliet has a vision of what is to come. This is significant, because it is the final time we will see them together alive. Conjuring such an image at such a time reiterates the way in which death haunts every scene in this play. It is mentioned so frequently that death is almost a lingering spectral figure on the stage itself. Later in this scene, Lady Capulet mirrors Juliet's vision by saying, 'I would the fool were married to her grave'.' Similar prophetic statements are uttered by other characters such as Mercutio, 'A plague on both your houses'; Romeo, 'I dreamt my lady came and found me dead' and Friar Lawrence, 'these violent delights have violent ends'. Shakespeare litters the play with images of premature death, reiterating at every point the doom which awaits.

Audiences expect death in tragedy. But that death, as Poole puts it, should be 'dignified' and 'exceptional'. Shakespeare builds towards the final scene and the deaths of the lovers with the constant, relentless layering of warnings and visions of the inevitable. In many ways, the fact that their deaths are fated, that they are written in the 'stars,' adds a level of exceptionalism and romanticism which they wouldn't otherwise have had. They are special - their deaths are supposedly serving a purpose. The Prologue suggests that their deaths will eventually end 'their parent's strive' and we may therefore see this tragedy as meaningful. It is tempting to suggest that, in a time when infant mortality was high and people were constantly forced to cope with the deaths of loved ones, a belief in fate and destiny, that there is a divine plan, was a comfort to people. Perhaps Shakespeare's vivid depiction of fate in action in the lives [and deaths] of the young, is an attempt to explore the purpose or futility of death.

Shakespeare's language

In the 1930s a literary academic, Caroline Spurgeon, wrote a hugely influential critical study of Shakespeare's language, called, somewhat unimaginatively perhaps, Shakespeare's *Imagery and What it Tells Us*. The central idea of Spurgeon's study was that Shakespeare's figurative imagery falls into groups or clusters and these clusters vary from play to play. Moreover, Spurgeon opined that these image clusters are the most important generators of the distinct mood and atmosphere of each play and also convey key thematic concerns.

However, since the 1930s Spurgeon's approach has been criticized and refined in various ways. There have been three main criticisms, the first of which is less obvious, the other two probably a bit more predictable: Firstly, as a pioneering female literary academic writing in the 1930s Spurgeon was constrained by decorum; hence she entirely ignored imagery to do with sex. Secondly critics have also contested her choices of dominant image clusters in each play, suggesting that alternative clusters are just as, or are even more, significant. Thirdly, other critics have gone a step further, disagreeing with the privileging of imagery above other features. Why, for instance, is imagery more significant than repeated single words [think of the importance of 'blood' in Macbeth or 'stars' in *Romeo and Juliet*] or other literary devices such as antithesis ['my only love sprung from my only hate']? What about the use of verse, and prose, and Shakespeare's bending and meshing of iambic pentameter with syntax?

Moreover, aren't characters also pretty important features of plays, especially in texts that are written to be performed on a stage by actors? Words, of course, matter, more than that they're crucial. But there's an old cliché that actions speak louder. Surely the action of the play is just as an important as the imagery. And so on. No doubt there's even a literary academic out there somewhere who'd argue that the real key to unlocking Shakespeare's plays is his use of relative pronouns or costumes. That might seem flippant, but the key point is to explore how are the dramatic elements work together in a play.

The depth and wealth of Shakespeare's language is profound, and *Romeo and Juliet* is certainly no exception. The language in this play is often very beautiful, but there are greater considerations than aesthetics. Shakespeare uses language to create dynamic, nuanced characters, and help the audience to genuinely feel their relationships with one another. An excellent example of this is the first meeting of Romeo and Juliet in Act I, Scene 5. The conversation in question takes the form of a shared sonnet between the lovers - a powerful way to establish these characters and the intensity of their connection. The sonnet opens with Romeo's first address to Juliet:

> If I profane with my unworthiest hand
> This holy shrine, the gentle sin is this:
> My lips, two blushing pilgrims, ready stand
> To smooth that rough touch with a tender kiss.

Immediately, we notice that Romeo's language has changed. He has moved from the language of a lustful youth, *'nor ope her legs for saint seducing gold'*, to one who literally worships Juliet as a holy being. Juliet is a 'holy shrine' and his lips are 'pilgrims'. In evoking contemporary religious ritual - kissing a relic or shrine in the hope of a miracle or blessing - Romeo marks out Juliet as being desirable, but also out of reach. She might be a person he can kiss, but is perhaps always going to be, in some part, an ineffable mystery to him.

This opening statement is very bold. But Juliet's strength of character is established immediately when she picks up on his metaphor and continues to carry it through into the next stanza:

> Good pilgrim, you do wrong your hand too much,
> Which mannerly devotion shows in this,
> For saints have hands that pilgrims' hands do touch,
> And palm to palm is holy palmers' kiss.

She chides him gently for his forwardness and reminds him that holding his hands in prayer would be a more fitting way to pay tribute to a holy shrine.

Quick-witted and creative with the physical comparison between a kiss and a prayer, she plays with the religious image. Juliet's language not only matches Romeo's it goes further by challenging his request. In Act I, Scene 1, Romeo's language was very complex and poetic, 'feather of lead, bright smoke' so the audience has already recognised the emotional depth of this character. When Juliet begins to spar with Romeo and clearly masters the sonnet form in this exchange, we recognise her own prowess and intelligence.

The sonnet gathers pace in the next stanza as the couple begin to alternate lines:

Romeo	Have not saints lips, and holy palmers too?
Juliet	Ay, pilgrim, lips that they must use in prayer.
Romeo	O, then, dear saint, let lips do what hands do.
	They pray; grant thou, lest faith turn to despair.

Romeo persists. He points out that both he and she, the pilgrim and the saint, have lips. But Juliet will not be moved and continues to resist his advances. It is significant here that a young virginal girl is knowingly using religious language with double entendres while being courted by a young man. Despite her earlier assurance to her parents that she will be mindful of their 'consent', she reveals herself as a more daring and decisive young woman than we have previously seen. The final two lines are a rhyming couplet, and it is significant that the pair share these lines between them. This final rhyme closes the sonnet with a kiss, and they appear to have reached a point of agreement. Juliet suggests that she will not 'move', but Romeo may still have his prayer 'grant[ed].'

| Juliet | Saints do not move, though grant for prayers' sake. |
| Romeo | Then move not, while my prayer's effect I take. |

In its structural harmony and complexity, the shared sonnet shows us a young love where both parties are perfectly in concert with one another. This is not just the kind of unrequited lust which Romeo felt for Rosaline. It is a meeting of true minds; a meeting, literally, of poets on the stage.

44

Of course, this is the central relationship in the play, so the shared sonnet is a rather grand way of framing their union. Shakespeare does, however, use similar tactics to present other key relationships in the drama. Romeo and Friar Lawrence have a mentor-mentee relationship which is akin to that between a father and son. This makes it a bond which is volatile, and the characters do not always agree. In Act III, Scene 3, The Friar must tell Romeo that he is banished from Verona. Romeo's frustration and anger with him is very evident,

> how hast thou the heart,
> Being a divine, a ghostly confessor,
> A sin-absolver, and my friend profess'd,
> To mangle me with that word 'banished'?

His description of the Friar as both a 'divine' and 'ghostly' implies that Romeo is uncertain of him. Shakespeare uses such antithesis frequently in the play, and, at this moment, it implies that Romeo doesn't know whether he can trust the Friar - he saw him as 'divine', but the advice he is now giving him makes him seem the opposite. Romeo's language here is an echo of the opening scene where his repeated oxymorons are a symptom of his youthful frustration and sadness. With the Friar, Romeo uses antithesis again, but this time the conflict is more serious - he is questioning someone who, before now, he absolutely trusted. This is compounded in the next few lines when the Friar laments at Romeo's stubbornness, 'I see that madmen have no ears'. Romeo retorts, 'How should they? When that wise men have no eyes'. The oxymoronic notion of a wise man who sees nothing mirrors the Friar's comment back at him, like an angry teenage son might argue with his father. This conversation is swift and heated, made more intense by the time pressures of Romeo's banishment, and exacerbated by Shakespeare's opposing imagery. Antithesis creates dramatic moments between characters which are highly emotive and create depth of understanding for the audience.

The same technique can be observed when Lord Capulet learns of Juliet's death, 'Death lies on her like an untimely frost/ Upon the sweetest flower of all the field' [Act IV, Scene 5]. Capulet uses the contrasting images of frost and flowers to highlight the unnaturalness of the death of one so young. He is a character from whom we have seen a broad range of emotions and extreme language, but at this moment he is using a clash of imagery. Just as in the case of Romeo's anger with the Friar, Lord Capulet's use of antithesis demonstrates his grief at Juliet's passing. Such juxtaposition can be seen at every level of this text, from minute vocabulary and imagery comparison, all the way up to the overarching themes. Famously, Juliet described Romeo as, 'my only love sprung from my only hate' in Act I, Scene 5, and thus Shakespeare's language simultaneously depicts powerful relationships whilst also emphasising the rift between families at the very heart of this play.

The playwright

Had we but the space and time [as well as the skill, the scholarship and, indeed, the inclination] we could, perhaps, provide an exhaustive account of the life and work of the world's most famous writer. After all, the Shakespeare scholar, James Shapiro managed to write a highly engaging account of just one year, albeit a monumentally creative year, in the bard's relatively short life.[6] On the other hand, very little information actually exists about Shakespeare's life; famously one of the only extant official documents is his will and its curious instruction to leave his wife his second-best bed. Of course, that gaping biographical vacuum hasn't stopped scholars, biographers and novelists; in fact it's invited them to jump right in and fill the gap with all sorts of colourful speculations. There's a snobbish and preposterous conspiracy-style story, for instance, that Shakespeare didn't really write his own plays, nor presumably all of his own poems.

But, we haven't the space or time for such fanciful speculations. What the can usefully be said about William Shakespeare [1564-1616] in a couple of pages or so? Firstly, that he was middle-class, grammar school educated, and that he didn't attend either of the great universities of Oxford or Cambridge. This fact partly accounts for the claim that Shakespeare couldn't have written his plays as, so the argument goes, he had neither the aristocratic life experiences

---

[6] Shapiro, *1606, The Year of Lear*.

nor the sophisticated education to do so, a claim unpleasantly whiffing of snobbery. How could a middle-class actor from the provinces write so brilliantly about kings, queens and princes and different times and cultures? Perhaps he read widely, observed keenly and used his prodigious imagination.

Secondly, at the tender age, even for Elizabethans, of just eighteen Shakespeare married an older woman, Anne Hathaway, who was twenty-six and already pregnant. This is a point to be borne in mind whenever Shakespeare is writing about star-crossed love or disinherited and bitter children - those born out of wedlock and therefore labelled as 'bastards' in his world.

Thirdly, Shakespeare was an actor and many scholars think he probably took roles, albeit relatively minor ones, in his own plays. He was a member of an acting group, called the Lord Chamberlain's Men, who had a theatre built to house their performances – the Globe theatre. Perhaps his plays were refined through the process of rehearsal.

Fourthly, Shakespeare was not only a highly successful playwright, but also a shrewd businessman. By middle-age he had become wealthy enough to buy the 'second largest' house in Stratford. By this time, his acting company had been promoted up to the top of the social ladder to 'The King's Men', with a royal charter and King James I as their patron. And so they had purchased a second theatre.

Fifthly, Shakespeare was a highly accomplished poet as well as a playwright. Writing a decent sonnet was considered de rigueur for an Elizabethan courtier. Shakespeare did not only write one decent sonnet, naturally; he wrote a sonnet sequence, a bigger and better and more sophisticated sonnet sequence than anyone has managed before or since, arguably. Comprising over a hundred and fifty sonnets, the sequence dramatizes the story of an intense love triangle, involving Shakespeare, a handsome young man and a mysterious dark lady.

Sixthly, Shakespeare is absolutely everywhere. He is the only writer whose work by law has to be studied in English schools. His poems and plays are read, studied and performed across the globe, from Australia to China, from India to Zambia, and have been translated into almost every major language, including Klingon[7]. Unsurprisingly, he's the best-selling writer ever. Estimates suggest that there have been over four hundred film versions of his plays.

Phrases and words Shakespeare coined are used every day by thousands, perhaps millions, of people, sometimes consciously and sometimes because they have become interwoven into the fabric of our language. And that's still not the be-all and end-all: His head appears on bank notes, cushions, cups and tea-towels [there is even a Shakespeare rubber duck] and he is a crucial part of the English tourism industry and British national identity. In this country alone, there are several theatre companies dedicated to his work, 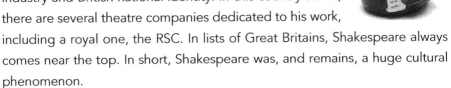 including a royal one, the RSC. In lists of Great Britains, Shakespeare always comes near the top. In short, Shakespeare was, and remains, a huge cultural phenomenon.

Some critics suggest that the boy from Stratford got lucky; his work spread over the globe because first the Elizabethans and then the Victorians explored and conquered much of the world and everywhere the English went they took Shakespeare along with them. But, even then, that doesn't explain why Shakespeare, rather than any other English writer, became so revered and ubiquitous.

---

[7] Apparently 'taH pagh taHbe' is Klingon for the very famous opening to a speech by Hamlet.

Shakespeare's world

Picture this: a happy, stable, highly ordered, hierarchical society in which each man and woman knows their place and, moreover, knows that this place has been rightfully assigned to them and fixed by God. And all things on earth are held together in a great, universal chain of being. Furthermore, this fixed and eternal orderliness reassuringly mirrors the fixed, eternal order of the heavens. As God rules the heavens so the monarch, God's representative, rules the earth. And the present monarch, Good Queen Bess, Gloriana, is a semi-divine virgin queen who has ruled peacefully for four decades. England is a bucolic, Edenic society in which an especially blessed race of men live harmoniously with each other and with nature. A demi-paradise, in fact. Recent religious conflicts between Catholics and Protestants have been consigned to history. The arts are blossoming as never before. Trade with the rest of the world is expanding and flourishing. Sending her ships out across the furthest seas, England is becoming a global super-power, bringing peace and prosperity for all. It is a veritable golden age. A merrie, merrie England.

The only problem with this enchanting picture is that it is, according to modern literary critics and historians, largely just that, a picture, a construct, a beguiling illusion. Whether Queen Elizabeth I's reign was ever a golden age is a matter of historical debate, but what is not really disputed is that by around 1595, the time Shakespeare was writing *Romeo and Juliet*, England was fast becoming a very different, swiftly changing, more turbulent and troubled country.

While it is true that English society had inherited the feudal idea of the Great Chain of Being, and with this ideological construct the idea that a static social order had been ordained by God, it is also the case that this sort of inherited thinking was being challenged vigorously on many different fronts. In politics, the power of the monarchy and the lords was coming under more democratic pressure to reform. Laws were changing in the same more democratic direction. Increasing trade was creating a newly prosperous mercantile class, especially in London. These merchants were growing rich and powerful and upwardly mobile, threatening the established aristocratic class. Increasingly Elizabethans were fashioning new identities for themselves, or re-defining themselves through their actions and possessions, their writing and artworks, rather than through their inherited family name or status. Science was evolving rapidly too, developing an empirical method that did not just accept inherited understanding of the word, but instead tested evidence objectively via repeated experimentation. At the same time, a range of humanist intellectuals were questioning some of Elizabethan society's fundamental principles. Meanwhile, Puritans were busily decoupling faith in God from loyalty to the church and to the monarch. England may have been relatively peaceful, but it faced the perpetual threat of invasion by Catholic Spain or France as well as potential insurrection from within, such as the Earl of Essex's revolt. On top of this, plague had swept through the country in the 1590s and would do so again in 1603.

Looking backwards a little way from the final years of Elizabeth's I reign we see the political turmoil of the reigns of Henry VIII and his short-lived immediate successors; look forward a decade and the Gunpowder Plot of 1605 swims into view, when Catholic conspirators tried to blow up parliament and assassinate the king. Cast our eyes a little further forward, and only a few decades after Shakespeare had written *Romeo and Juliet* and barely suppressed tensions in English society bubbled up, erupted and the country broke into violent civil war.

While there is no doubt there were many tremendous achievements of the Elizabethan age, including Shakespeare's own work, historians' investigation of the treatment of women and ethnic minorities, closer examination of the appalling living conditions of the poor, inspection of Elizabethan society's penal system and spy network and its most popular forms of entertainment, has uncovered a more complex, nuanced picture. Fine-grained analysis of many different aspects of Late Elizabethan society reveals it to be a much more unstable, dynamic, dangerous and fascinating place - a maelstrom of clashing ideas and beliefs. Shakespeare's age was a cultural furnace that fired his imagination and provided the power for his plays.

Critical commentaries on acts & scenes

Our commentaries on these the acts and scenes of the play aim to provide both a broad overview of each Act and a closer, more fine-grained inspection of some of the most significant scenes. They are not intended to be completely comprehensive. That would take a much longer book and even then there's an inexhaustible amount that could be written about the play. Instead, our focus will sharper and more concentrated, looking at critical aspects of each Act, such as how the dramatic action unfolds, how characters develop and how Shakespeare uses language.

At times we will make reference to other plays by Shakespeare. It is not expected that pupils will necessarily know these plays, but a little knowledge about them can help to clarify and amplify what Shakespeare is about in *Romeo and Juliet*. From time to time, we also draw on some concepts about tragedy, particularly the seminal work of Aristotle. Similarly, rather than have a long, worthy introductory section to this book about the socio-historical context of Elizabethan England, we have sprinkled this sort of context throughout these commentaries and also through our explorations of character. As Professor Peter Barry writes in *Reading Poetry*, a 'generalised and open-ended notion of social or historical context' is not a useful tool for examining a specific text, because 'contexts of that limitless kind are like oceans' by which individual texts 'will inevitably be engulfed'[8]. Though Professor Barry is writing about poems, clearly the same holds true for any literary text. A little context goes a long way.

---

[8] Peter Barry, *Reading Poetry*,

Act One

Shakespeare's Prologue to *Romeo and Juliet* immediately warns the audience to anticipate tragedy; the 'ancient grudge' between the two rival households – the Montagues and Capulets – will inevitably lead to the deaths of the play's 'star-cross'd lovers'. This truth-telling sonnet draws us into a world where love and hate, life and death and fate and free will jostle together in inharmonious

proximity. As in many of Shakespeare's tragedies, such as *Macbeth* and *Hamlet*, Act I, Scene 1 disrupts hierarchical expectations, by not starting with the protagonists but, instead, with a chaotic brawl between the servants of the two rival households, exposing how deep-rooted this hatred is. Although Romeo's cousin Benvolio attempts to 'keep the peace', he exacerbates the 'hate' of Tybalt, Juliet's cousin and the play's main antagonist. Despite the Prince's demand that such 'pernicious rage' is ended, Shakespeare highlights how the dark desire for revenge can overshadow the potential for peace. It is the men of each household who fuel the animosity, reflecting the overwhelming dominance of patriarchy in shaping societal values. Arguably Shakespeare uses this fracas to criticise Elizabethan expectations of masculinity, particularly the chivalric code of martial honour, which valued reputation and physical prowess above emotional and moral intelligence.

Following the street scuffle, Benvolio discovers Romeo in a state of 'despair' due to the unrequited 'love of a woman', who we later learn is Rosaline. Romeo knows what it means to 'live dead', an oxymoron that foreshadows his later destiny. In plays what happens off-stage is often as significant as what happens on-stage: Rosaline never actually appears in the play, a detail that contributes to Shakespeare's exploration of gender inequality and an overwhelming culture of objectification.

Shakespeare shifts perspectives in Act I, Scene 2. Here Romeo's melancholy is contrasted with the determination of his love rival, Paris, who seeks Lord Capulet's permission to marry Juliet. There is a symbolic parallel between Rosaline's unheard voice and Juliet's controlled upbringing; neither are given any say. Capulet speaks on his daughter's behalf, assuring Paris that he is 'honourable', but Juliet is not yet 'fourteen' and thus 'too ripe to be a bride'. This horribly casual dehumanisation reduces Juliet to a piece of fruit to be consumed and signals how a woman's worth was narrowly determined by virtue and virginity. Capulet welcomes Paris to attend his party, before sending a servant to distribute invitations to selected guests. Conveniently, Benvolio and Romeo pass by the servant, who asks for their assistance in reading the guestlist, since his illiteracy prevents him from doing so. This encounter reinforces the thematic significance of fate; if the paths of these characters had not crossed, Romeo may never have attended the party and met Juliet. However, seeing Rosaline's name on the list, Romeo vows to 'go along' to the party, eager as ever to win her love.

It is not until Act I, Scene 3 that the audience meets Juliet. The stagecraft here is important. Shakespeare introduces the Nurse, who has cared for Juliet since she was a 'babe', before Juliet's mother, Lady Capulet. The contrast between the Nurse's affection and her mother's detachment is stark. Lady Capulet's personal ambition sparks her suggestion that despite her tender years Juliet 'think of marriage now' and look for Paris at the party. The contradictory attitudes of Lord and Lady Capulet towards Juliet's marriage is significant, exposing their lack of emotional connection and anticipating the repeated personal and political conflicts that shape the play's action. For Lord and Lady Capulet, marriage is based, rather conventionally, on status rather than love.

Act I, Scene 4 brings us back to Benvolio and Romeo, now joined by their friend Mercutio, masked and ready for Capulet's party. Both Romeo and Mercutio have had strange dreams, with Romeo certain that 'this night's revels' will lead to 'untimely death'. The audience knows from the Prologue that this love story is destined to end badly, thus Romeo's ominous premonition reinforces the deliberately ambiguous question of how far fate is within or beyond human control.

Despite attending the party for Rosaline, famously, when he sets eyes on Juliet in Act I Scene 5, Romeo instantly falls in love with her. In this scene, Shakespeare draws on the conventions of metatheatre, making us question how far our identity is always a performance: The power-hungry Lord Capulet opens the party like an actor, theatrically inviting his guests to enjoy the occasion. His welcome to the 'gentlemen' contrasts with his demeaning invite to the women, asking the 'mistresses' to dance. Shakespeare's symbolic inclusion of 'masks', more commonly employed in his comedies [such as the

famous masked ball in *Much Ado About Nothing*], indicates duplicity is afoot. Perhaps the masks also suggest that superficiality is at the heart of many Elizabethan relationships, including that of Romeo and Juliet.

Capulet's welcome is followed by Romeo's instant infatuation. His 'heart' feels 'love' for her 'true beauty', as 'she hangs upon the cheek of night/ Like a rich jewel in an Ethiope's ear'. Written in the heartbeat rhythm of the iambic pentameter, Romeo's speech is rich in rhetoric and laced with romantic imagery, such as the references to 'light' and 'snowy dove'. This mode of speaking constructs him as the archetypical Elizabethan lover, more in love with his own flourishing descriptions than the woman he claims to have such overwhelming affection for. The play's title and tragic ending, combined with romanticising interpretations offered in many film adaptations [such as director Baz Luhrmann's modernised 1996 version], often lead us to overlook the shallow origins of this relationship. The simile, dehumanising Juliet as the 'jewel', for instance, values her appearance rather than her character, while the comparison to 'an Ethiope's ear' perhaps reflects the racial tensions that pervaded Elizabeth culture.

Romeo's declaration of love is interrupted by an enraged Tybalt. Hearing Romeo's voice, Tybalt realises that a Montague 'villain' has crashed the party. Although Capulet demands Tybalt remain 'quiet', the antagonist bristles under this constraint. Tybalt's behavior suggests how an obsession with proving one's martial honour can outweigh common sense and integrity. Crucially Act I, Scene 5 allows Shakespeare to critique constructions of love, gender and toxic masculinity. Following Tybalt's outrage, Romeo approaches Juliet, seemingly having already forgotten his love for Rosaline. Shakespeare's cross-cutting approach between Romeo and Tybalt anticipates the cinematic possibilities of this scene and encourages us to consider whether the protagonist and antagonist are as dissimilar as first appearances suggest. Addressing Juliet as his 'dear saint', describing his lips as 'two blushing pilgrims', Romeo makes her his object of worship. Perhaps the metaphorical 'pilgrims' insinuates an overriding lustful desire, as Romeo uses religious terminology as a form of seduction rather than respect. Juliet, having been presented as innocent in

Act I, Scene 3, now gives her 'pilgrim' a kiss without hesitation, showing no maidenly pang of conscience about her flirtatious approach to this 'sin'. Structurally it is significant that they exchange just fourteen lines – the length of a sonnet – before the first kiss. Whilst this may suggest that they are romantically destined for one another, it also shows how rushed their relationship is; they are still essentially strangers. Shakespeare's use of the sonnet form and rhyme scheme, with both characters rhyming 'this' with 'kiss' to capture their blossoming mutual feelings, cleverly echoes the Prologue, the play's first sonnet. Thus, whilst the party setting and the light-hearted wordplay between Romeo and Juliet sets this moment up as one of unbridled joy and romance, their love is already overshadowed by a reminder of their tragic destinies.

Juliet is not simply a one-dimensional, passive recipient of Romeo's patriarchal objectification. She is quick-witted and, although she passively lets Romeo kiss her, she instigates their second kiss, before suggesting that he 'kiss by the book': this could signal her lack of experience, but could also be a subtle suggestion that Romeo may have learned how to kiss from a manual and thus has an adequate but unoriginal technique! Such an interpretation is supported by Romeo's continual 'performance' of being a lover, expressing his emotions in a self-consciously poetic manner rather than authentically.

The amorous connection between Romeo and Juliet does not last long. The Nurse interrupts, summoning Juliet on behalf of Lady Capulet, before revealing to Romeo that Juliet's mother is 'the lady of the house'. Romeo's speech is reduced to fragments, his previous rhetoric disintegrating as he realises that 'his life is [his] foe's debt'. Shakespeare scatters imagery of commercial value throughout the play - the 'debt' a reminder of what a heavy price all the characters will play for letting the 'ancient grudge' dominate their lives, prompting the audience to evaluate what the most important values in life and love really are.

Once the Nurse has delivered the truth to Romeo, she lets Juliet know that 'His name is Romeo, and a Montague'. Perceptively and poignantly, Juliet realises that her 'grave is like to be [her] wedding bed', a simile that

foreshadows her death alongside Romeo in the same church that the Friar secretly marries them. Unlike Romeo, Juliet continues to talk in rhyme: 'My only love sprung from my only hate!/ Too early seen unknown, and known too late!'. The juxtaposition of 'love' with 'hate' and 'unknown' with 'known' expresses her conflicted emotions alongside Shakespeare's suggestion about the irreversible consequences of long-held antipathy, particularly when younger generations are indoctrinated to believe that the 'enemy' should be 'loathed'.

Juliet suggests that it is now already 'too late' to go back, hinting, before the end of Act I, that she and Romeo will attempt to remain 'star-cross'd lovers', despite the fact that their 'death-marked love' can only end in tragedy.

Act Two

Act II opens with the return of the Chorus, who outlines the events to come. While the Chorus is not always reliable, here it picks up two elements of early modern marriage debates central to the play. First is tension between 'old desire' and 'young affection'. Traditionally parents had arranged marriages for their children, such as the Capulets are organising between Juliet and Paris, with financial security, alliances between families, and maintaining social classes the priority. It was hoped that the betrothed [who might barely know one another at the time of engagement] would come to love one another during marriage. By Shakespeare time, the younger generations had begun to rebel and to consider love a priority before marriage took place. While the play is named after the main romantic couple, suggesting that it sides with the young lovers, the concerns of the older generation are not ignored; Romeo's tendency to be 'beloved' and 'love again' – his affection switching suspiciously rapidly between Rosaline and Juliet – reminds us that head-over-heals love-at-first-sight can be an unreliable basis for marriage.

The second element is the power imbalance between the two generations and, within those generations, the sexes too. While both young men and young women struggle against their parents when making choices about their future, young women also have to battle against strict patriarchal roles and expectations. Romeo 'may not' have access to profess his love or to appeal to the Capulets for Juliet's hand in marriage, but Juliet's means are 'much less' again. The generational power imbalance is shown in the need of both young lovers to gain support from members of the older generation to assist them in their courtship. However, while Romeo can go to someone outside their families [Friar Lawrence], Juliet must keep within her home and gain the support of her nurse.

Act II of the play tracks the couple's journey from their second meeting to their hasty marriage. After the Chorus speaks, we are transported to a street near the Capulet home. Romeo has fled from his friends and family after the masque and scaled a wall into the Capulet orchard to meet again with Juliet.

The famous balcony scene where the lovers pledge their hearts and hands to one another follows. Thereafter, the action turns to the engagement of Friar Lawrence and the Nurse to assist the young pair in getting married. The wedding itself takes place in secret in Scene 6. Let's look more closely at the perception of love within and across the generations, and the recruitment of older allies to challenge conventions.

Magic, potions, and love as madness

Scene 1 is dominated by the mischievous wordsmith Mercutio. The younger generation's own inner conflicts around love are showcased as Mercutio taunts his vanished friend as a 'madman,' which he suggests is synonymous with being a 'lover'. Mercutio mocks love as a form of possession. Using magic as a metaphor, he declares that Romeo is in the grip of his 'humours' [loosely equivalent to what we would now call 'hormones'] and is behaving according to the stereotypes or rituals to which all lovers succumb. Love, he implies, is emasculating. Romeo has become little more than a spirit, the embodiment of 'a [lovesick] sigh,' and can be 'conjured' to do almost anything at a woman's bidding. Bawdy jokes abound with Mercutio suggesting that Romeo may only act like a man in the sense that he can be 'raised' to 'stand' within his 'mistress' circle' [a play on the idea of a magic circle and a heretosexual man's response to a desired woman's privates] but no longer has any mind of his own. Romeo is, in the eyes of his friend, has been softened and enslaved by love.

Distinct from, but not dissimilar to, Mercutio's response to Romeo's heartsickness is Friar Lawrence's. Scene 3 picks up the magical analogy via its setting in the Friar's cell, where 'herbs, plants, and stones' are being organised as part of the Friar's apothecary trade. The play's tragic ending in both death and belated peace is foreshadowed in his handling of a 'small flower' where both 'poison' and 'medicine' reside, and the potential to convert 'virtue' to 'vice' and vice-versa. Romeo confesses his new love for Juliet, prompting an exasperated lecture from the Friar that summarises the older generation's anxieties about trusting love as a foundation for marriage. The speed with which Romeo's affections have switched, the Friar observes, proves that 'young men's love then lies/ Not truly in their hearts, but in their eyes.' Like Mercutio, the Friar suggests that Romeo is weak but, unlike Mercutio who tars both with the same brush, he suggests that weakness comes from 'doting, not…loving.' The Friar distrusts Romeo's lusts not love itself.

He further notes that men's weakness is their own, not the fault of women – 'women may fall, when there's no strength in men'. Here he shows greater maturity and wisdom than Mercutio, reminding Romeo that responsibility for Original Sin [the Fall of Man] lay with both sexes, not women alone. He too wonders if this is another fleeting infatuation of Romeo's – 'thy love did read by rote' – but while Mercutio sees it merely as fuel for sex jokes, the Friar is willing to support the inevitability of the partnership in the hope that a marriage between Romeo and Juliet can be used to end the 'ancient grudge' and 'turn your households' rancour to pure love'.

The generational and gendered power gaps are illustrated clearly in this scene and the one that follows as Romeo has the agency to move freely in society to seek the Friar's assistance and arrange for his marriage to take place. His authority is notably less than the Friar's, since the latter plans to shape the future of two families not merely his own. Juliet, by contrast, cannot even leave her home alone and must acquire the assistance of the Nurse first, before sending the latter out on her behalf.

Emphasising the divide between the public sphere dominated by men and the private sphere to which the women were confined, we do not see Juliet liaise with her nurse. Instead we see only the Nurse, escorted by Peter, meet with Romeo. She too is suspicious of Romeo's affections and cautions him against 'weak dealing' – courting Juliet with the intention of bedding her rather than marrying her. Reflecting her more limited role in society, the Nurse has no ambitions to make peace between the warring houses but is open-minded about the younger generation's desire to match love with necessity and prioritises Juliet's happiness over the Capulets' more practical desires for a suitable match. Juliet, she notes, has confided in her that she sees Paris as a 'toad' and that she 'pale[s]' at the idea of marrying him - strongly suggesting that a happy marriage is not on the cards with her parents' selected partner. Having evaluated Romeo herself as 'gentle as a lamb,' 'honest,' 'courteous,' 'kind,' 'handsome', and 'virtuous', the Nurse is content to conspire with her charge and arrange the marriage Juliet has chosen for herself.

You may also want to consider how class intersects with gender here. Does the Nurse have the agency to resist the commands of her young charge, who [as a noblewoman] outranks her working-class guardian or not?

Love by rote?

The balcony scene, the most famous within the play and among the most famous in Shakespeare's canon, has been written about so extensively it scarcely needs discussion here. It is, however, worth marking some of the language within the scenes shared by the couple in this act and how this plays into the concept of a generational revolt. Although Juliet is relatively powerless within her own family and in wider society, she is presented here as

strong-minded and much more decisive than Romeo himself. Her interrogation of 'what's in a name' is an 'assault on social rigidity and received wisdom' [Donkor: 'Character Analysis: Romeo and Juliet,' 2017]. As Michael Donkor notes, Juliet proposes a radical transaction that cuts through a number of patriarchal conventions. First, she makes the first offer of her hand in marriage, before Romeo 'didst request it', rejecting the tradition of her father dictating to whom she should be married. Second, she offers herself to Romeo if he will give up his 'name,' reversing the convention that a woman's name and identity be subsumed into her husband's after marriage. Third, she controls Romeo's advances. Her repeated reminders that her kinsmen will kill him test his courage in approaching her and grounds his grand gesture in their chilling reality. She then cuts through his hyperbolic and cliched declarations of love, seeking plain truth and commitment. While Romeo speaks of conquering 'stony limits,' 'twenty swords,' and farthest sea[s]' to claim her love, Juliet demands straight answers and repeatedly edits his effusiveness with stern logic: 'swear not by...the inconstant moon...lest thy love prove likewise variable'. She also commands the pacing of their love affair, noting that it is 'too rash, too unadvised, too sudden' to pursue immediately. Instead, she insists they both sleep on their encounter and that, if Romeo feels as she does in the morning, he makes concrete plans for their marriage rather than more dramatic gestures.

By the time we reach the final scene in this act, there is a greater sense of balance between the two lovers, with each professing their love succinctly and in equal measure before Friar Lawrence.

What do you think about the way the younger and older generations seem to perceive love and marriage? Are Romeo and Juliet naïve for wanting to marry for love despite their families' enmity? What about Friar Lawrence and the Nurse – what do make of their behaviour? Are the elder Capulets and Montagues short-sighted themselves in being unable to move past their historic fallings out when marriages have a long-tradition of being used to heal divides between warring families? Is love 'enough' to be the basis for a marriage or is there a bigger picture to consider as well?

Act Three

Shakespeare's plays all last for five acts, and the third act is often regarded as the 'pivot' scene - the part of the play where things start to unravel most quickly and the action is most crucial to the plot's eventual journey.

Romeo and Juliet is no different. At the end of Act II, both lovers were about to marry in perfect union - Friar Lawrence sends them off to become 'two in one'. By the end of Act III, however, Mercutio is dead, Tybalt is dead, Romeo's chances of getting away with marrying Juliet are also dead and Juliet's father has set a wedding date for her to marry Paris. Romeo has gone from being 'a virtuous and well-governed youth', as he's described by Capulet in Act I, to 'an old murderer'.

How quickly fate changes. And how quickly Shakespeare tells us about it. Capulet points this out in Act III, Scene 4: 'Things have fallen out, sir, so unluckily,/ That we have had no time to move our daughter'. Paris tells us, too, that, 'These times of woe afford no times to woo'. These quotes help us to focus on a key aspect of this 'pivot act' - the sheer speed at which everything falls apart like a sodden wedding cake.

The deaths of Mercutio and Tybalt happen right at the beginning of this Act. They are two separate deaths and carry with them two separate 'character histories'. The two characters are mourned by different people and represent different groups within the play, with Mercutio of the Prince's 'house' and Tybalt a Capulet and Juliet's cousin. However, it might be helpful to think about both of their deaths as one big tragic bloodbath that directs the rest of the course of the play. Or, rather, it allows the tragedy to unfold, as has been anticipated in the Prologue.

Mercutio and Tybalt are killed within fifteen lines of each other, which is a pretty extraordinary pace of death. There's a sense of uncomfortable irony in the fact that Benvolio opens the line 'brave Mercutio is dead' with 'O Romeo,

Romeo' - and even if you haven't read the play before you'll probably recall this line as one of the most famous, spoken by Juliet from her balcony - 'O Romeo, Romeo, wherefore art thou Romeo?' How quickly those few yearning words stop being associated with love. Now they are bringers of dreadful news, reflecting the
tragedy to come.

After they have both died, the scene ends with a lot of characters on stage  who are either witnesses or who have dashed in to see what all the fuss is about. As well as Benvolio, the Prince, Capulet, Montague, Capulet's wife, Montague's wife there are generic 'citizens'. Together they try to make sense of senseless violence, with Benvolio adopting the tone of the narrator of an epic poem, with heavy metre and portentous full rhymes: 'Here lies the man, slain by young Romeo,/ That slew they kinsman, brave Mercutio'. Normally the first syllable in iambic pentameter would be weak, but here it is stressed – '**here lies** the **man, slain** by **young** Romeo'. The immediate, intimate horror of 'here' he lies is emphasised. Both the characters and the audience are told to get right up and personal with the horror of what's in front of them, foreshadowing how the final scene will see them all physically gathering around the bodies of Romeo and Juliet.

When the other characters decide that Romeo must be banished, the scene ramps up quickly. The sense of rushing finality shows in the increasing numbers of perfect end-rhymes - 'fly' and 'die'; 'Montague' and 'not true'; 'strife' and 'life'; 'proceeding' and 'a-bleeding'; 'will' and 'kill'. Shared between Montague and the Prince, the conclusion of the scene forms fourteen lines, which makes up a sonnet. However, the rhyme scheme is not what we'd expect from a Shakespearean sonnet. Instead, it follows in couplets. This is much more final, more in-your-face, like the beating of a terrible drum. The formal order of full rhymes is being imposed on the disorder and chaos of the scene that has gone before. We leave this scene absolutely knowing that the terrible fate awaiting Romeo – which, of course, we already know about from the sixth line of the whole play- has now been articulated in some way by other characters. The characters may think it's just banishment; we know otherwise.

Having focused on this scene in general, we'll turn our attention now to two elements of Shakespeare's technique that are used throughout the whole play, but which are particularly pronounced in this act - the use of foreshadowing and the emphasis on the importance of words. Specifically the language that the characters use in this act constantly lets slip foreshadowing and portentous images of death. Hence Shakespeare is able to speed up how much information is compacted in the play, which means that the audience hears information which makes them think *yes, I already know that.*

Look at the opening of Scene 3. At first glance it might be overlooked due to its brevity and lack of dagger-y action. There are lots of lines in this play that could sum up the overall plot, but Friar Lawrence's opening - 'thou art wedded to calamity'- does the job pretty well. Everyone is, somehow, wedded to calamity, because the tragedy of the titular characters not only affects everyone, but implicates them too, since the teenagers died on their families' watch. Perhaps the audience is also 'wedded to calamity', as we are bound by duty [and maybe ticket prices] to watch all the way through to the tragic end.

Romeo is now in hiding, being comforted [or not, as the case may be] by 'adversity's sweet milk, philosophy'. He and Friar Lawrence are alone, speaking about the terrible nature of the word 'banishment', which is described with awful hyperbole. The word 'banishment' itself causes Romeo immense pain: 'How hast thou the heart... to mangle me with that word 'banished'?' Friar Lawrence offers him 'armour to keep off that word', positioning the word itself as an attacker. There's an emphasis here on the damage that words can do, as Romeo seems more afraid of the threat of the word rather than the reality of banishment that he faces. But, then, he realises that action is better than just sitting around talking. 'Hang up philosophy!' he cries, 'unless philosophy can make a Juliet... it helps not, it prevails not. Talk no more.' Romeo also makes references to aspects of time that confuse us, as he says here that he is 'an hour but married', whereas Juliet said in the previous scene that she is his 'three-hours' wife'. For Romeo - and for us - time is being shortened, compacted, pushed on.

This emphasis on language and on naming aligns him with Juliet, who in Act II famously ruminates 'What's in a name? That which we call a rose/ By any other word would smell as sweet'. To the Friar, Romeo asks 'In what vile part of this anatomy/ Doth my name lodge?' The words 'my name' could very easily be replaced by the words 'this poison'; both a name and a medicine is deadly. Could the play make it any more obvious here that having the 'wrong' surname means bad luck for everyone? This isn't the only place where both Romeo and Juliet refer, unknowingly, to their own fate. For example, Juliet's opening soliloquy in the second scene of this act keeps circling back to 'night', which appears nine times in 31 lines. For her, night represents the consummation of her marriage. But, oddly, she also refers to it as the 'sober-suited matron all in black', which seems unnecessarily portentous for someone imagining a night of passion with her betrothed.

The narrative in these scenes motors along at a swift pace. In Scene 4 Capulet is making 'a desperate tender/ Of my child's love' to Paris only a few lines after he has acknowledged 'Well, we were born to die'. By Scene 5, Capulet is threatening Juliet that she will go 'to church a' Thursday/ Or never after look me in the face'- which, of course, she doesn't [a further exploration of this scene can be found in the section on the Capulets]. Shakespeare makes the narrative more compact by the characters constantly referring - without knowing it - to their own death. They're not just dying at the end, but they've already died in the Prologue, too, and every time they mention their own death without realising. Indeed, Romeo has no idea how bad the future is when he says, in Scene 3, 'Banished!/ O Friar, the damned use that word in hell;/ Howling attends it'. It's ironic, given that later he will take his own life, which according to church teaching at the time would commit his soul to the same 'hell' he's referring to here.

However, the 'damned' use lots of other words in this play as well, including the word 'love'. This word is used a staggering 175 times in the play overall. Love trumps 'death' which only appears 75 times. In Act III alone, 'love' is mentioned 31 times, and 'death' 24. This leaves us with some questions, which based on your knowledge of  the play you might like to answer for yourself. What are our characters, and the audience, destined for? Is the play telling us that no matter what happens, no matter how 'canker'd' the fateful language given to the protagonists, love will win? Or is death stronger, no matter how many times Romeo and Juliet try and keep it away by talking about love? Which actions and words do we assign greatest strength to in this text - that of the repeated word 'love', or the actions of killing, mourning, and avenging? How trapped are we too, the audience, by the language and references the characters are forced to make, their fate made inescapable by their talking it into existence? That, we'll leave for you to decide.

Act Four

Act IV conveys the tragic consequences of Mercutio's death and Romeo's revenging murder of Tybalt. In Act IV, Scene 1, love rival and antihero, Paris, tells the Friar that he wishes to 'haste' his marriage to Juliet, with the repetition of 'haste' conveying both his urgency to make Juliet his wife and also the 'haste' with which all characters have acted: the marriage of Romeo and Juliet; Romeo's rash killing of Tybalt; the immediacy with which Capulet disowns his daughter. Arguably Shakespeare reinforces here the dangerous consequences of instinctive, thoughtless actions, driven by emotions rather than rational thought.

Juliet interrupts proceedings between Paris and the Friar. She responds to Paris enigmatically, acknowledging his request that they marry next Thursday with the fatalistic 'What shall must be'; the modal verbs 'shall' and 'must' suggest Juliet's resignation regarding her future and her awareness that such a wedding is an impossibility, with the generalised 'What' also referring to the fate that she and Romeo 'must' face. Juliet undermines Paris' imperative to 'not deny' her 'love' by confirming that 'I love him'. Unlike Paris, the audience know that Romeo is the subject hidden behind her impersonal pronoun 'him'. Once Paris exits, Juliet begs for a 'new-made grave', preferring to die rather than 'live an unstain'd wife to [her] sweet love'. The metaphorical 'unstain'd' reinforces how a woman's worth is defined, in the play, by her virginity and purity, while the 'grave' foreshadows her imminent death in the same church that she married Romeo. The Friar has 'hope' to save their relationship and, as Juliet follows the Friar's orders to 'go home', taking with her a 'vial' to make her appear dead, she considers the 'price' that she must pay for her actions. This imagery of commerce is used throughout the play.

Juliet remains the focus in Act IV, Scene 2, performing the role of obedient daughter by claiming that she 'repent the sin/ Of disobedient opposition', having previously refused to marry Paris. Echoing Capulet's disdainful description of her in Act III as a 'Disobedient wretch' could convey Juliet's attempts to appease her father, who had previously threatened to let her 'hang, beg, starve, die in the streets'. Alternatively, by inverting his speech pattern, Juliet subtly undermines his authority. Seemingly Capulet has forgotten his rage, informing Juliet that she must marry tomorrow so he can 'have this knot knit up'. The 'knot knit' image, on the surface, refers to marriage, but it is also an ominous reminder of how tangled the fates of all the characters are. Capulet feels satisfied that 'this same wayward girl is so reclaim'd'. His impersonal treatment of Juliet here reflects how entrenched his patriarchal beliefs are and how his own reputation drives his decision-making.

Act IV, Scene 3 sees Juliet make perhaps her most powerful soliloquy. She

 begs the Nurse and her mother to 'now be left alone'. They follow Juliet's wishes and her mother commands that Juliet 'Get... to bed, and rest', a tragic premonition, perhaps, of her impending eternal sleep. Juliet's soliloquy is full of rhetorical questions, as she considers 'if this mixture' will 'not work at all?' and continues to share her doubts before drinking the vial. She even considers whether the Friar might have administered a 'poison' to mask his own role in marrying them. Juliet is left with 'a faint cold fear' that 'thrills through [her] veins' and 'almost freezes up the heat of life'. The extended imagery of temperature further foreshadows her fate and suggests Juliet's own subconscious awareness that her relationship with Romeo is surely doomed.

Juliet's terror causes her to imagine waking up with the dead, seeing 'the mangled Tybalt' and subsequently ending her own life by dashing out her 'desperate brains'. The personification here illustrates her frenzied state of mind and the violent imagery, so far associated with the male characters from each household, may reflect Shakespeare's subversion of such stereotypical masculinity and a belief that men, like women, should express emotions such as 'rage' and being 'distraught'.

The tension spills into Act IV, Scene 4, with Juliet's swallowing of the sleeping potion juxtaposed with Capulet's confident optimism that the 'second cock has crow'd'. The combination of portentous signals further forewarns of a tragic fate. Capulet impatiently calls up to the Nurse, notably listed before his "wife", suggestive of his awareness that the Nurse has played a more significant role in Juliet's upbringing. In addition, the impersonal noun wife' reinforces his association of marriage with status rather than love.

We will focus our close analysis on the final scene of Act V, Scene 5, in which Juliet's 'dead' body is discovered. As in Act I, when Juliet is first introduced to the audience, the Nurse appears first. Assuming that Juliet is 'sound... asleep', she light-heartedly teases Juliet that once she is a 'bride', Country Paris will allow her to 'rest but little'. The dramatic irony of the Nurse's innuendo in anticipation of the wedding highlights how little even she understands Juliet's true character and the extent to which the truth can be hidden behind layers of duplicity. Nevertheless, the Nurse's care for Juliet is clear. Hysterically she cries 'lady! lady! lady!... My lady's dead!'. The Nurse only refers to Juliet once by her first name here, using titles instead such as 'mistress', 'lady', 'madam' and even 'bride'. The listing of respectful, but impersonal terms highlights Shakespeare's exploration of the nexus of Elizabethan gender politics, class division between the Nurse and her 'lady', and the extent to which status defined an individual above character or moral values.

The Nurse's exclamations attract the attention of Lady Capulet. She plays the role of grieving mother, lamenting 'O me, O me! - my child, my only life!' The repeated, emphatic first-person pronouns betray her self-interested reasons for grieving, grieving at she has lost. More sympathetically, her melancholic cry for 'my child' and 'only life' echoes Capulet's earlier revelation that the couple had lost many children before Juliet's arrival. Her birth and survival reinforces Shakespeare's fascination with fate and the extent to which individuals can or cannot control their own destinies.

Lord Capulet joins the scene of trauma. In stark contrast to the fragmentary cries of the Nurse and Lady Capulet that 'she's dead', he talks with immediate rhetorical ease, noticing that 'she's cold' and that 'Death lies on her like an untimely frost'. Capulet's imagery parallels Juliet's soliloquy, suggestive of the 'cold' familial bonds and a reminder of how Capulet's insistence on her marriage appears to have caused her death. Shakespeare's personification of 'woful time' also embodies the concept of destiny, indicative of the limitations that individuals have over their 'time' on earth as well as the length of that the 'ancient grudge' has continued. Capulet's personification of death, which 'Ties up [his] tongue', further illustrates how life and death are more powerful than human understanding. Capulet's rhetoric is at odds with his grief, a reminder of his performative approach to social roles: rather than letting himself be vulnerable to raw emotions he retreats into a role.

The Friar soon enters. Feigning ignorance by asking whether 'the bride' is 'ready to go to church', the Friar distances himself from Juliet, choosing the same impersonal marital noun 'bride' as the Nurse used earlier. Capulet shows the Friar where Juliet lies alongside 'death', now this 'Flower as she was' has been 'deflowered'. By applying the concept of 'deflowering' – traditionally associated with taking a bride's virginity – grotesquely to death here, Shakespeare reinforces Capulet's warped patriarchal control and how his tyrannical control of his daughter only leads to disaster. Ironically Capulet's 'son-in-law' is not Paris, but Romeo. The familial language foreshadows the imminent fates of the play's 'star-cross'd lovers'. The juxtaposition of 'living' and 'death' [a contrast repeatedly referenced in the play] in his speech mirrors Juliet's current state of still 'living' but appearing to be dead.

Lady Capulet, meanwhile, laments that they have lost the 'one, poor one, one poor and loving child'. The chiasmus, 'poor one, one poor', is particularly interesting, syntactically signalling how Juliet is trapped within a her 'poor' fate. Shakespeare returns to the imagery of commerce and value: whilst Juliet is economically rich, her upbringing provided her rich emotional connections; indeed, being starved of love from her parents arguably influenced her rash decision to marry Romeo immediately. Paris continues to bemoan the fact that they will experience only 'love in death'. In another ironic twist, this will indeed be the fate awaiting Juliet and Romeo, not Juliet and Paris.

The Friar instructs the family to remember that 'heaven' has chosen her and that 'she's best married that dies married young'. This damning verdict on marriage reflects a sense of disillusionment; in a world fraught with conflict and injustice, a life in 'heaven' as a 'fair maid' [the thumping dramatic irony unmissable] is a preferable destiny to earthly suffering. Turning the 'wedding cheer' into a 'sad burial feast', the Friar and the family leave, determined not to anger the 'heavens' and to follow 'their high will'. Personifying heaven allows the Friar and the other characters to shy away from responsibility, blaming, instead, forces beyond human control or understanding.

With the main characters gone, only the wedding musicians remain. Peter, a Capulet servant, attempts to persuade them into playing. They refuse, engaging instead in light-hearted wordplay that contrasts with the gravity of the previous dialogue. This almost humorous conclusion to Act IV, Scene 4, as the musicians show little care or empathy for Juliet's fate, is a final embodiment of how transient and ultimately forgettable each human life is. As W.H. Auden later noted, suffering often takes place 'while someone else is eating or opening a window or just walking dully along'.

Act Five

We all know how this play ends. In the final scene of Act V, Romeo and Juliet lie dead in the tomb. The Prince tries to impose some sort of order on the assembled company and asks:

> Seal up the mouth of outrage for a while,
> Till we can clear these ambiguities
> And know their spring, their head, their true descent.

On the surface of it, the Prince is there to provide some answers, like the quickly narrated 'whodunnit' explanation at the end of TV murder mysteries. However, it's not quite as simple as that. How did we come to this, the Prince asks? What is the 'true descent' of these horrors? What were the root causes? Who claims agency, or responsibility, for these events?

And how have things come to this? At the beginning of this final act, Romeo doesn't know yet that Juliet has been found 'dead', but is told by Balthasar. Grieving, Romeo goes to the Apothecary to find a poison with which he can end his life. Meanwhile, Friar John hasn't sent the letter to tell Romeo that Juliet is not, in fact, dead. Friar Lawrence sets off to her tomb immediately so that he can wait for Romeo. In her tomb, Juliet is not alone. Her husband-that-wasn't, Paris, has come to throw 'flowers' on her 'bridal bed'. Romeo enters and threatens Balthasar that if he tries to interrupt him he will 'tear thee joint by joint'. Balthasar leaves, but Romeo finds and kills Paris.

Now alone, Romeo drinks the poison after a confused, anguished soliloquy about Juliet, her beauty and the 'abhorred monster' of death. He kisses her and dies. Balthasar and Friar Lawrence arrive too late, but just in time to see Juliet wake up and tell her that 'Thy husband in thy bosom there lies dead'. She kills herself with Romeo's dagger. At this point, everyone else rushes in. Collectively they decide what has happened to the two teenagers is so horrendous that the two families must make tentative amends.

As far as play endings go, it does what it says on the tin. Whereas the play started with a brawl in public, it ends in the Capulets' tomb. The play has moved from public to private, from a political brawl to intimate, personal tragedy. The text starts by showing the physical life and vitality of men in Gregory and Samson, but it ends showing the all-encompassing power of death. Plotlines are wrapped up and there's the faint glimmer of a happy[ish] ending rising from the ashes, as the lovers' deaths may finally bring peace and harmony for the warring families. Our tragic heroes have martyred themselves on the altar of everlasting love, but darker and less noble characteristics lurk beneath the heroic surface.

We'll start with Romeo's reaction to finding out that Juliet is dead. As is the case elsewhere, he acts rashly. Whereas Capulet opines about mortality and the afterlife at length on learning of Juliet's 'death', Romeo moves straight to putting the gears into action to ensure his own demise. Perhaps he is in shock at learning so quickly that his dream of 'joyful news at hand' has been ripped apart by Balthasar's news that 'Her body sleeps in Capel's monument'. However, this speed of reaction seems strange. He's just found out that his wife is dead. Why doesn't he take just a few minutes to process that information? Could it be that his dreams from the beginning of the act- 'I dreamt my lady came and found me dead' - have unconsciously prepared him? Is it the hand of Fate, or the supernatural, that plants these images in his dreams and speech and pushes him firmly towards the Apothecary to get the poison that will kill him?

This question of agency is brought into sharp focus by the conversation between Romeo and the Apothecary. Conveniently, the latter was in earshot of Romeo whilst he was describing the insides of his shop. The Apothecary is reluctant to sell Romeo the poison, telling him that 'Mantua's law/ Is death to any he that utters them'. So, Romeo knows that by pushing this sale he is potentially lining this man up for a death sentence. He tells the Apothecary that he's so poor that surely death would be welcome:

> Art thou so bare and full of wretchedness,
> And fearest to die? Famine is in thy cheeks,
> Need and oppression starveth in thy eyes,
> Contempt and beggary hangs upon thy back

While it would be easy to write off this treatment of the poor on the basis that Romeo is 'not himself' and that he is 'grieving', arguably he's actually *very much* himself here, and that this is completely in-keeping with his actions earlier in the play, where he goes to grand lengths to do what feels is 'just'; he kills Tybalt in an eye-for-an-eye gangland-style murder. We already know that he tends to act in his own interest. For example, he turns up at Juliet's bedroom window without her knowledge to pursue his own desire to see her. Surely, if Shakespeare wanted us to see Romeo as a tragic, noble hero, he would not have included this scene with the Apothecary. Romeo bullies someone weakened by poverty to give him what he wants, regardless of the death sentence it'll give the other man. Shakespeare could so easily make this scene different, with a willing chemist who hands over the drugs. The Apothecary could even just point out that attempting suicide is a crime and that Mantua would sentence *Romeo* to death if his attempt fails. But no - we learn that the seller would also be condemned to the same punishment and that Romeo is therefore complicit in knowingly making it possible that this man might die.

So, who's responsible in this Act for ensuring that the tragedy can happen, as promised to us by the Prologue? Does the Apothecary have to fulfil Romeo's request? Whatever the answer, the Apothecary makes a choice - he accepts the immediate benefit of 'gold, worse poison to men's souls'. Like so many others in the play, he prioritises immediate gain over long-term moral cleanliness.

Whilst it is true that the Prologue locks the play onto its course, it's also true that the characters' fate is locked in by their own choices. Even some of the smallest choices that are made in the play show an impulse towards self-preservation. We learn in Scene 2 of this act that Friar John couldn't get a messenger to take the letter, 'So fearful were they of infection'. This is probably referring to the real-life plague, and because of it the letter can't be delivered - a plot twist that turns a heroic, triumphant win for young love into a road to certain death. Paris' fate is also sealed by the fact that he follows his own desires in breaking into Capulet's tomb, against the rules. You'd think that it would be acceptable for Paris to visit the tomb of his fiancée who was found dead on their wedding day, so why does Shakespeare make his behaviour so secretive? He creeps in with his page, telling him 'Hence, and

stand aloof... for I would not be seen'. However, this version of Paris, breaking the rules to do what he *really wants* to do, fits in more neatly with an Act that shows the consequences of characters acting in their own interest. Romeo kills him in order to achieve his own much-wanted death. Neither Paris nor Romeo have won here, despite both trying to pursue their own desires.

So, which characters are most responsible for the events of Act V? Is it the messengers, who put their own health over the need for the letter to be delivered? Or the Apothecary, who takes the money even though he surely knows Romeo will use it to commit suicide and send his own soul to hell? Is it Romeo, who turns to death as a way out of every situation - both to escape his own sorrow at Juliet's death, but also to dispense with the problem of Paris interrupting him in his efforts?

Ironically, it is Paris who interrupts Romeo in the tomb, since Romeo had technically interrupted Paris earlier on in the play by marrying Juliet before Paris got the chance - but it's also a good dramatic opportunity to further underline that Romeo makes the choice to kill Paris, who doesn't exactly threaten mortal harm when he just says that he'll arrest him - 'I do defy thy conjuration/ And apprehend thee for a felon here'. Romeo didn't even know for sure that Paris was the man Juliet was 'meant' to marry, for he said 'I think/ He told me Paris should have married Juliet./ Said he not so? Or did I dream it so?'. He kills him anyway, for he stands in the way of the task ahead. In modern lingo, we'd say that response wasn't proportionate. It might seem, then, that Romeo has become a violent nihilist, unencumbered by guilt and ready to take the world down with him in revenge for taking away his Juliet. Alternatively, perhaps Romeo is just one of many characters who look after their own interests, and it's the selfishness of the characters in this act that combine to produce the eventual tragedy that befalls our stage.

Quite a lot of bad choices made by our characters, then. But what do they actually say about guilt, and how are these events reported by the characters when we reach the final scene of the play? Friar Lawrence finds Paris dead and comments, 'Ah, what an unkind hour/ Is guilty of this lamentable chance!' He also notes that 'A greater power than we can contradict/ Hath thwarted our intents'. Even though it would be obvious to the audience that Paris has been killed by a human being, the Friar frames his death as being down to the 'greater power', that 'an unkind hour' is 'guilty' of the crime. When Juliet wakes up, she talks about the poison killing her as if she is passive, as opposed to saying that she will choose to take it - 'Haply some poison doth yet hang on them/ To **make me die** with a restorative'. When that doesn't work, she asks the dagger to release her from life - 'there rust, and **let me die**'. Capulet sees the dagger in Juliet's chest and says it must be a mistake, not a deliberate act - 'This dagger hath mista'en... And is mis-sheathed in my daughter's bosom'. Now that the full tragedy has been laid out at their feet, the remaining characters all frame events passively, as if they have been foisted upon the victims, accidental, not actively sought. So who takes responsibility for these events?

This act doesn't necessarily help us answer these questions. Nor is it meant to. The play as a whole tussles with the problem of agency. Are the characters answerable to the universe, the spoiler at the start of the play, and also the fact that their stories are written by the playwright before they are even born in the rehearsal room? Are we meant to see them as helpless victims of the playwright's fatal pen? Or are they young hotheads who don't live long enough to learn their lesson, who infect the other characters by their relentless search for meeting their own needs?

The chasm of responsibility that their deaths create is in some way answered by Shakespeare's ending of the play. Here the Prince's authoritative closing of the stage indicates that for now, order and agency will preside. Perhaps he is meant to represent divine intervention; the God-figure shaking his head at the endlessly errant ways of his human creation. Whatever he is, he certainly shows that a return to 'official' justice will follow - 'some will be pardoned and some punished'. Having delineated the devastation caused by feuding families taking matters into their own hands, the play closes with a promise that the Prince will take responsibility. Through his words, the foggy ambiguity around important questions of agency will, for once, be cleared.

Critical essays on characters

There are dangers in providing exemplar essays. Inadvertently, such exemplars can close down the space for your own thinking and encourage uncritical regurgitation of an essay's content in examinations. Our essays were not written in timed, examination conditions. They are not intended to be examples of what an examination board would expect from any student in those conditions. Primarily, our essays are not designed as model answers. Moreover, fundamentally, we don't believe there can be only one model answer to any literary question. The best English Literature essays express pupils' own critical thinking and opinions, informed by engagement with other readers and guided by their teachers. Hence our aim in the following essays is to provoke, stimulate and inform your own thinking about the play's major characters, not to replace your thinking. We aim to make you reflect more critically on the characters' and their roles and functions in the play.

Hopefully, our essays will make you think again, perhaps even make you think differently. Sometimes you may also encounter readings with which you disagree. Good; so long as you can explain and justify why you have come to different conclusions. Whether you mostly agree with our interpretations or not, these essays should, however, provide plenty of information you can digest, ponder, alter, reformulate and contest in your own words.

Remember when you are writing about characters to try to lift your perspective above the character-level action of who said what and who did what to the author-level perspective of why these words and actions are significant.

Romeo

Alpha Romeo

According to Aristotle, a tragic hero faces an unhappy fate, usually due to a fatal flaw in their character, a hamartia. Romeo, certainly, is destined for a tragic ending and Shakespeare conforms to some classical conventions: the play ends in the deaths of the main characters; the antagonist, Tybalt, disrupts the path of true love; there is a range of meaty themes – love, revenge, conflict and hate. However, Shakespeare also subverts his audience's expectations, particularly through his portrayal of a protagonist, Romeo, whose hamartia is, perhaps, simply being too impulsive. Does Romeo deserve to be condemned after his anger overrides rationality and he murders Tybalt? Or is he still just a teenager, whose fate has always been determined by his family's 'ancient grudge'? Shakespeare invites multiple interpretations of Romeo's character: on the one hand, a victim of familial animosity; on the other, a rash, lust-driven, perhaps selfish, individual. Ultimately, Romeo must surely be more than simply a puppet in the hands of fate; that would make him too passive and pitiful a character for us to care much about. Fundamentally, he is a more problematic, complex individual, more in love with the idea of falling in love than with Juliet herself.

Romeo first appears on stage performing as a perfect Petrarchan lover; melodramatic, self-absorbed, wallowing in his melancholy at Rosaline's rejection. Petrarch, a popular source of inspiration for Shakespeare and contemporaries, praised lovers who celebrated their objects of affection as a 'goddess' or 'lady', suggesting love to be all-consuming and often a form of exquisite suffering. Romeo shares his woes as a sonnet, his oxymoronic 'brawling love' and 'loving hate' reflecting his own contradictory feelings. It is his own rhetoric which Romeo seems to truly love. The juxtaposition of 'hate' and 'love' not only reflects Shakespeare's deeper criticism about how the 'hate' between families can prevent 'love' from blossoming, but also how Romeo's own 'love' is more a 'serious vanity' for himself and his desire to fulfil the role of a lover.

Just a teenager in love

Another interpretation of Romeo, however, could be more forgiving. Shakespeare's protagonist is a teenager, lacking the experience to not feel 'madness' and a 'choking gall' when facing rejection. Romeo's metaphorical

suggestion that 'love… is a smoke raised with the fume of sighs;/ Being purged, a fire sparkling in lovers' eyes' foreshadows his subsequent 'burning' passion for Juliet as well as their 'purged' lives; love, like fire, has the potential to be 'sparkling' but also to destroy. Romeo is, fundamentally, simply an inexperienced adolescent, seeking love because his upbringing was full of hate. He claims to be 'not Romeo, he's some other where'. This use of third-person emphasises his self-indulgence but also his youthful struggle to forge an independent identity.

Shakespeare continues to portray Romeo as the hapless Petrarchan lover as Act I continues. Having intercepted Capulet's servant and crept into the Capulets' party with Benvolio, Romeo focuses blindly on his pursuit of Rosaline, although any details about Rosaline her remain scarce. Romeo continues to indulgently muse on what love means, believing that it is 'too rough,/ Too rude, too boisterous,' like a rowdy boy and that it 'pricks like thorn'. The triple adjectives 'rough', 'rude' and 'boisterous' could be equally applied to a teenager and his description of love, therefore, could also be a description of his own self. Shakespeare does not portray Romeo as an outwardly insecure character, however. As soon as he sees Juliet, Romeo immediately forgets his supposedly deep, unrequited love for the off-stage

Rosaline.

Shakespeare's depiction of Romeo is almost comedic at this stage. Hyperbolising Romeo's reaction to Juliet's beauty, the apostrophe 'O, she does teach the torches to burn bright!' reflects the earlier fire imagery and

draws on the Petrarchan trope of describing the subject of love as a goddess. The rhyme of 'bright' and 'night', reflects the light and dark motif repeated throughout the play, suggesting perhaps the shades of Romeo's own character. The imagery is conventional romantic stuff, compounded by Romeo's dehumanising simile of Juliet as a 'rich jewel'. Whilst Romeo could be interpreted as a passionate lover - repeating his admiration for Juliet's beauty, comparing her to a 'snowy dove trooping with crows' - it is a startlingly sudden and seemingly shallow display of affection.

Shakespeare implies Romeo is in love with his performance of love above all else. Personifying his 'lips' as 'two blushing pilgrims', he elevates Juliet to a 'saint', despite still never having spoken with her. Romeo recycles imagery from earlier in Act I, suggesting that Juliet will 'smooth that rough touch with a tender kiss. Repeating 'rough' and 'tender', there is a sense that Romeo is still playing the role of the lover, first with Rosaline, now with Juliet. Hence Shakespeare uses Romeo as a vehicle to question the nature of love and the experience of falling in love. In addition, the interaction between the two characters raises questions about how authentic the identities we present to others ever truly are, particularly during our turbulent years as young adults.

As the party ends, Romeo yearns for Juliet. In Act II, Scene 2, he sees her on the balcony outside her bedroom. Here Shakespeare presents Romeo as consumed with lust rather than love, evident through his objectifying attitude to Juliet's beauty. His soliloquy compares Juliet to the 'fair sun' which can 'kill the envious moon'. On the surface, this metaphor suggests that Juliet is the centre of Romeo's universe, although this formulaic Petrarchan ideal, dehumanising Juliet, is based on their single brief encounter. In addition, it reflects the influence of his family's feud on Romeo's imagination; even when thinking of love he thinks in terms of violence and cosmic conflict. Romeo continues his hyperbolic praise, suggesting that the 'brightness of her cheek would shame those stars'. Again this repeated light and dark imagery reflects the various conflicts in the play, including that between different sides of Romeo's own character. Romeo is hiding at a distance, so a cynical audience may question how far he can see her 'cheek'. He also desires to be a 'glove' upon her hand, indicating that his feelings are based on physical attraction. Performing the Petrarchan lover, Romeo compares Juliet to a 'bright angel', which foreshadows her later fate, set for heaven', but also shapes her into being something otherworldly, suggesting that their love is elevated by rhetoric rather than grounded in reality.

By Act II, Scene 3, having met Juliet twice, Romeo visits the Friar about their 'holy marriage'. The tone is not one of celebration, however, unlike the engagements in Shakespeare's comedies, such as *Twelfth Night* or *Much Ado About Nothing*. Rather, Romeo urgently needs the Friar to 'marry [them] today' without even telling the Friar how they made exchange of vow'. Shakespeare portrays Romeo as behaving like the director of his own play, attempting to orchestrate fate in a manner reminiscent of Prospero's magical interferences in *The Tempest*. Is Shakespeare criticising such rash behaviour or perhaps the arrogance of 'playing God', taking fate into one's own hands? Romeo does not even not even use Juliet's name when speaking to the Friar, describing her as the 'fair daughter of the rich Capulet, a choice of adjectives that are patriarchal and depersonalised.

Romeo's controlling behaviour continues in his conversations with the Nurse in Act II, Scene 4. His demanding tone suggests an obsessive orchestration of the scene. He instructs the Nurse, 'there she shall at Friar Lawrence' cell/ Be shrived and married'. Juliet is again left nameless, reduced to the impersonal pronoun. Whilst it could be argued that Romeo is so besotted that he needs to seal his love immediately, such impetuousness reveals again his less favourable nature: directive, impulsive and almost aggressive. He treats the conversation like a commercial transaction, offering the Nurse a reward 'for [her] pains'. Romeo's plan works, however. By Act II, Scene 6, they are married. There's no extensive ceremony, although ignoring the Friar's advice to 'love moderately', Romeo believes that 'sorrow' cannot remove 'the exchange of joy'. The Friar notes how 'A lover may bestride the gossamer' - the delicate references to 'light' and 'gossamer' reminding the audience how fragile their relationship is. Romeo focuses on love as a concept and suggests that Juliet 'sweeten with thy breath/ This neighbour air'. Again, his compliments to Juliet echo well-worn Petrarchan tropes, as Shakespeare implies that Romeo, due to his youthful desire to 'direct' his own fate, has entered a marriage of 'imagined happiness'.

A new Romeo?

During the confrontation between Tybalt and Mercutio in Act III, Shakespeare conveys a turning point in Romeo's character. Romeo is the voice of reason, reminding Tybalt that he has 'never injured' him and does, in fact, 'love' him 'better than' Tybalt 'canst devise'. Romeo appears more heroic, at least for a modern audience, an advocate of 'love and peaceful resolution to the 'ancient grudge'. However, the audience knows the self-interested reason for his desire to avoid fighting, since, by marrying Juliet, Tybalt is now Romeo's in-law. However, Romeo's words are ignored. In a fateful stage direction, Tybalt goes 'under Romeo's arm and stabs Mercutio'. Mercutio's famous dying line, a 'plague o' both your houses!', further undermines Romeo; it is both the families that are cursed. Even Romeo recognises now that he is 'fortune's fool'. His failed attempts to prevent the fight, before rashly taking revenge and killing Tybalt, illustrate how one individual cannot so easily overturn entrenched animosity or stop cycles of violence from rolling destructively onwards. His naive actions also highlight how young and impulsive he still is.

Shakespeare reinforces the impossibility of controlling fate in Act III, Scene 3, when the Friar warns Romeo that he will be banished. Romeo reacts immaturely to being banished, claiming that 'more courtship lives/ In carrion-flies than Romeo'. His use of third person again suggests a mental unravelling, as he disconnects from the version of himself who committed murder and is now sentenced to life away from Juliet. Meanwhile his comparison to the deathly 'carrion flies' foreshadows his own fate and reflects his dissatisfaction at losing his status. It also reinforces Romeo's theatrical character, a young man who has yet to establish who he really is – lover, peacemaker, revenger, friend, son. Romeo repeatedly questions why he is 'banished', seeing a life without Juliet as 'ghostly'. His inability to control his emotions is again evident.

Romeo's grief spills into his final conversation with Juliet. His repeated imagery of 'light and light' and 'dark and dark' signifies his 'woes' and his own conflicted character. His reliance on existing Romantic tropes emphasises the struggle he has to find an identity. Juliet uses 'light' in the literal sense, warning that morning is arriving, and Romeo echoes her language to express his heightened emotions. It is Juliet who shows foresight about their destinies, imagining Romeo 'dead in the bottom of a tomb'. In contrast, Romeo continues to drown in the melancholy of the moment. He suggests that 'sorrow drinks our blood', this vampiric personification serving as a portent of their doomed love. Unusually for an eponymous character, Romeo is then absent for a whole Act, as Act IV focuses on Juliet and her plans to appear dead. With Romeo off-stage, his power and status are diminished. Thus Shakespeare demonstrates how quickly an individual can be forgotten, using Romeo to convey the transience of human existence.

Romeo, of course, returns in Act V, ready to meet his downfall in the final scenes. Act V, Scene 1 begins in Mantua, where Romeo has been banished. Shakespeare references Romeo's recent dream, the play's repeated dream imagery reflective of how far their attempt at love is from reality; it is nothing more than a 'Strange dream'. Romeo's vision foreshadows how his 'lady… found [him] dead'. Hence his foreboding dream is like a dress rehearsal for his later discovery of Juliet, when he, too, 'breathed such life with kisses'. The tone shifts after the messenger, Balthasar, delivers news of Juliet's death. Romeo's reaction, tinged with sadness, is heated by lust, as he determines to 'lie with [Juliet] tonight'. Whilst this foreshadows his own death, it also hints at his desire to 'lie' sexually with her, his actions driven not by deep connection but by his physical desires. Romeo's melodramatic response continues as he seeks a 'dram of poison' from an apothecary, his focus already turned from

Juliet to the stage management of his death.

When he discovers Paris already at the tomb, Romeo continues to act on impulse, landing himself with more blood on his hands. Emptily he promises Paris 'a triumphant grave', before his grief returns to Juliet, noticing how 'her beauty makes/ This fault a feasting presence'. His sole focus is on objectifying her 'beauty', with the adjective 'feasting' underscoring his hunger for intimacy. Romeo remains obsessed with Juliet's appearance, observing how 'beauty's ensign yet/ Is crimson' in her 'lips' and 'cheeks'. While the dramatic irony is clear - the audience know that this is a literal reference to the fact that she has not surrendered to 'death's pale flag' – the line also conveys Romeo's stereotypical attitude towards Juliet as an object of appreciation for the male gaze. He maintains his dramatic rhetoric right until his death, commanding his 'lips... The doors of breath' to 'seal with a righteous kiss'. His metaphor suggests that his overwhelming physical attraction to Juliet, combined with his desire to play the part of the tragic lover, ultimately drive his actions and final decisions.

Once Juliet wakes up and *'Falls on ROMEO's body, and dies'*, Shakespeare uses a cyclical structure by reintroducing the Prince. It was, of course the Prince who delivered the words of warning in Act I. The cyclical structure reflects how Romeo and Juliet are more than characters; they are constructs to convey Shakespeare's warning about the tragic consequences of 'hate', as 'all are punish'd' as a result of the 'ancient grudge'.

No great tragic hero

Romeo, then, is no great, awesome tragic hero like Macbeth or Othello, whose respective hamartias [namely, 'vaulting ambition' in the former's case and the 'green-eyed monster' of jealousy in the latter's] catalyse their dramatic downfalls. Rather Romeo is a victim of fate. If he has a hamartia, it is his impulsive adolescent behaviour. The play never give him the space or time to develop from being a lustful, passionate youth, doomed by his desire to control a fate that – like his own sense of identity – lies beyond his control and understanding.

Juliet

Juliet is everywhere

Juliet is one of Shakespeare's most famous characters, immortalised in an afterlife rich in Oscar-winning adaptations for film, ballet and opera. Juliet is quoted in the Disney adaptation of *Princess Diaries*, a coming-of-age film about a teenage girl finding her way through the changes of adolescence. A passage from one of Juliet's soliloquies was even read out at USA President J. F. Kennedy's funeral after his assassination.

Juliet is, in fact, everywhere. There's so much out there on our ubiquitous, world-famous, eponymous hero - how do we even start sorting through all of the stacks of information? Well, perhaps this description of her as a 'hero' is as good a place to start. This essay will explore what kind of 'hero' Juliet might be, using different theories of how tragedy works to assess how we might see her in the context of the play.

Shakespeare was a playwright who was well-versed in the classical tragic heroes of ancient Greece and Rome, but there are lots of ways in which Juliet  diverts from classical conventions. For a start, tragic heroes are normally men, and are not normally thirteen-year-old girls [although modern literature has corrected that imbalance, thankfully]. Aristotle - the seminal Greek theorist on tragedy who lived in the 4th century BC - tells us that the tragic hero is desperately trying to do the right thing in a scenario where it's impossible to do so. He also theorises that tragedies are made by their plots, not by their characters. However, audiences would surely be likely to disagree with the philosopher. Without a compelling hero, surely a tragedy would be tragic in name only? Surely, without such the spontaneous, vivacious and headstrong Juliet - noting that her surname 'Capulet' literally means headstrong – the lovers' deaths wouldn't make such an awful ending? [That's 'awful' in the sense of horribly tragic, rather than not very good, by the way.]

Interpreting and creating Juliet

As with many of his most successful plays, Shakespeare started by taking his characters from other sources. Studying why authors change things from their sources can be a really great, quick way of identifying the aspects that were most important to them. Linda Hutcheon neatly sums up the process of adaptation by pointing out that 'adapters are first interpreters and then creators'.[9] Shakespeare makes some very specific changes to Juliet when he inherits her from Arthur Brooke, who wrote *The Tragicall Historye of Romeus and Iuliet* in 1562. The first is that Shakespeare's Juliet is younger. In Brooke's poem she is almost sixteen, and it should be said Romeo [or, as he's actually called in this version, Romeus] is also very young - he points out that on his 'tender chin, as yet, no manlike beard there grew'. However, in Shakespeare's version Juliet is only fourteen, which we are told six times. Meanwhile, Romeo's age isn't mentioned. Shakespeare *interprets* a girl fuelled by the impetuousness of youth, and he *creates* one that is even younger, perhaps to heighten her vulnerability and innocence.

So, Shakespeare made a conscious decision to make his hero younger than even his source tells us - indeed, she's the youngest female main character in any of his plays. Among Shakespeare's female tragic heroes, Juliet also has the third longest part. It's notable too that Shakespeare made such a young girl a bride. Whilst royals and ultra-high nobility may have been married off young for political gain, and the legal age that one could get married was 12, most people in the 1500s would have married in their mid-twenties - not far off the average marriage age in the 1930s. Therefore, an Elizabethan audience

---

[9] Hutcheon, *A Theory of Adaptation*.

would have also felt that Juliet is very young, both to have married herself to Romeo but also to be married off to Paris. Sidney, an Elizabethan poet rather overshadowed by the fact that he was publishing just before Shakespeare came along on the scene, thought that 'high tragedy' shows us the 'uncertainty of this world' exposing the 'weak foundations' that prove to be our undoing. Perhaps, then, Juliet is a tragic hero because she is too young a foundation to sustain the weight of reconciling two families, too young to make her marriage a force for good.

The fact that Juliet is surrounded by women much older than her emphasises her separation from the 'pack'. For example, her only confidante is her Nurse, who is much older. An only child, Juliet lacks siblings and/or friends of a similar age. Mostly she is shown on stage in private spaces, having enclosed conversations with those who are familiar to her already. The scene where she meets Romeo is the notable exception. Unlike Romeo, she doesn't have a big scene in public and she's not involved in any public brawling or duelling. Romeo is liberated by the fact that he can crash house parties where he's not welcome, whereas Juliet is trapped within her parents' house. In fact, it's arguable that an oft-neglected aspect of Juliet's character is how lonely she

must be. She is a child marooned in an adult world, a world not only uninterested in her tender years but actively ignoring her age. So perhaps we can empathise with her sense of urgency when calling Romeo to their

marriage bed - 'O, I have bought the mansion of a love/ But not possessed it, and though I am sold,/ Not yet enjoyed'. Isn't this part of wanting to belong more wholly to groups of adults she sees acting out these institutions of family? She is too young to know that there is more to the empty mansion after it's been 'possessed' - she doesn't see past the 'enjoyment'.

The 'mansion of a love' is an interesting metaphor for Shakespeare to use in this context. A 'mansion' is a large house where a lord might reside. Now teenage Juliet has one, and it's huge and empty, with her shut outside. To be in charge of a 'mansion' is a domestic image that a woman of greater years might be expected to assume in Elizabethan culture, but, like so much else in the play, Juliet has neither the age nor the experience to fully take charge of it. Perhaps Juliet's tragedy is that she can never quite understand or be in control of her environment, emphasised by Shakespeare's alterations to her age; perhaps what we see on stage is the result of her trying to wrestle with adults and forces beyond her control in a 'tragedy of miscalculation'.

This sense that she's 'playing at' adulthood further isolates her from the other characters, but links her to Romeo who often seems to be performing parts he's imagined. When the Nurse tells her that she should probably just go ahead and marry Paris, she cuts her last attachment to a support network, given that she's been cast aside by her parents [see more of this in the 'Capulets' section] and is separated from her husband. If Aristotle says that our tragic hero is just trying to do the right thing, then the play underlines how it is impossible for Juliet to do so; an inexperienced thirteen-year-old girl who has lost almost every champion has no way to navigate the slippery and dangerous world of Verona. Persistently Juliet is positioned as alone, separated from the comfort of others.

One of the symptoms of this yearning to escape the youth in which she's trapped is Juliet's remarkable sense of haste all the way through the 'two hours traffic of our stage'. Whereas the action of Brooke's poem lasts for nine months, Shakespeare's play squeezes the action into just five days. The haste of Juliet's decisions mirrors this new world of speeding towards the tragedy at the end of the play. Juliet opens Act III, Scene 2 thus: 'Gallop apace, you fiery-footed steeds… such a wagoner/ As Phaeton would whip you to the west and bring in cloudy night immediately.' She asks 'Come, night, come, Romeo, come, thou day in night… Come, gentle night, come, loving black-browed night'. So breathless is she to have Romeo come to her bedroom sooner that she circles around the same words, punctuated by endless, gasping caesuras.

She's always in a rush, is Juliet. But so too is the plot, racing towards the end that's been fated since the beginning. If Aristotle says that it's the plot more

than the character that creates a tragedy, then Juliet complicates things. She actively pushes the plot forward, presciently threatening her own death multiple times. Even the fact that she thinks it's a good idea to 'play dead' -as if that were the most reliable plan in these circumstances - is a sign of how she is unwittingly jumping the gun. Is it perhaps, then, that her status as a 'tragic hero' relies on her haste? Perhaps her hurry to get everything done is her Achilles heel, her fatal flaw, her 'hamartia'.

Juliet and her Romeo?

This essay hasn't sought necessarily to give you the crib sheet for understanding exactly and indisputably which box Juliet should fit into. The decisions that Shakespeare made in *interpreting* his source and *creating* the Juliet that we know today led to a character full of ambiguity and conflict. However, it's important to make a last point: where is Romeo in all of this [apart from in the 'Romeo' section of this book, of course}? Surely everything that applies to Juliet also applies to her lover.

Well, absolutely. To an extent. However, it's Juliet that is made *more* specific in Shakespeare's adaptation, whilst Romeo is made *more* ambiguous. Whereas Brooke tells us that 'Romeus' has lovely curly blonde hair and is too young to grow a beard, we don't really learn much about his appearance in Shakespeare's version. Nor do we know how old he is. Juliet, on the other hand, is given a fleshed-out age, her family is more dramatically developed and although Romeo has three soliloquies, Juliet has a whopping nine. Romeo may have 'top billing' in the name of the play - 'The excellent and conceited tragedy of Romeo and Juliet' - the play's ending places her very firmly on centre stage, 'For never was a story of more woe/ Than this of Juliet and **her** Romeo'. With a greater focus on young, hasty Juliet, arguably the play channels Aristotle's tragedy of plot *through* a character made far too young to shoulder such weighty burdens.

The Montagues

The Montague family is one of the two warring houses in *Romeo and Juliet*. An unidentified historical discord between the Montagues and Capulets spurs the two families into repeated public conflicts in the playworld's present day. Verona's beleaguered Prince complains that both houses are equally to blame: 'Three civil brawls, bred of an airy word,/ By thee, old Capulet, and Montague,/ Have thrice disturb'd the quiet of our streets.' A more nuanced picture, however, emerges from the action of the play. While the Montagues are given fewer named characters, fewer lines, and overall less attention than the Capulet family, as spectators and readers we nonetheless obtain a sketch of them as the more peaceful of the two clans, a closer-knit family, and one able to consider a future without conflict from the outset – though the latter cannot be attained until Lord Capulet reaches out to make peace in the final scenes.

Evidence for the Montagues as the less antagonistic of the sparring families is established in the play's opening scene. It is two Capulet servants, Sampson and Gregory, who instigate the brawl: Sampson makes an insulting gesture [biting the thumb] at Abraham and Balthasar, Gregory goads Abraham in offering to 'quarrel' and continues to taunt the Montagues' servants when they refuse, until Sampson demands they 'draw' swords and the fight erupts in physical violence. The arrival of Benvolio Montague and Tybalt Capulet reinforces the idea that the Capulets are the antagonists. While Benvolio draws his sword to separate the combatants and tries to broker peace, Tybalt declares he 'hates the word [peace]' and launches into a parallel attack. The arrivals of Old Capulet and his wife and Old Montague and his wife further confirm the Capulets as the primary troublemakers. Old Capulet, arriving first, immediately calls for his sword and Lady Capulet intercedes only out of concern for her husband's ability to fight – 'a crutch, a crutch! Why call you for a sword?'. By contrast, when the Montagues arrive and Old Montague too calls for his sword, Lady Montague grabs hold of her husband and insists he 'shalt not stir a foot to seek a foe'.

Similar patterns of behaviour occur throughout the play. Lady Montague not only prevents her husband from fighting, but professes herself keen to keep her youngest son away from the battles of his elders. She is, she declares, 'right glad...he was not at this fray in Act I, Scene 1, suggesting she has hopes of a future where Romeo may not need to engage in such disputes. Romeo himself echoes this hope when Tybalt, who recognised Romeo when he snuck into the masked ball, challenges him to a duel in Act III, Scene 1. 'Good Capulet', he protests as he refuses the challenge, 'which name I tender as dearly as mine own – be satisfied'. Having secretly married Juliet, Romeo intends to make peace with the Capulets, regardless of his family's prior hostility to them. His elected pacifism is showcased when Mercutio accepts Tybalt's challenge in Romeo's place and the latter urges Benvolio to help him 'beat down their swords' to restore quiet to the streets. The Capulet family's insistent combativeness is presented in contrast to the Montagues endeavours to 'scape a brawl', primarily through Tybalt, who not only seeks to start a fight with Romeo but also accepts Mercutio's challenge and sees the fight through to Mercutio's death, wounding him 'under [Romeo's] arm' so determined is he to continue the quarrel.

It is notable too that Montagues tend to seek the cause of each new spat, looking to learn how it came about and how it might be avoided, and show willingness to take responsibility for their own misdemeanours. The would-be peace-maker, Benvolio, often acts as reluctant spokesman for events and, through his tales, the Montagues openly acknowledge when the fault lies with their House. In contrast, the Capulets frequently seek to lay blame upon, and demand harsher penalties for, their enemies.

In addition to their less aggressive depiction, the Montague family is presented as less fractured and more sensitive to one another than the Capulets. Both Lady Montague and her husband are shown to be concerned about Romeo's whereabouts and state of mind in Act I, Scene 1. With the servants' spat dealt with, Old Montague's attention turns to the tearful and secretive behaviour of his youngest son. He tells Benvolio, who has also noticed his cousin's private grief, that 'both myself and many other friends have sought to discover 'whence [Romeo's] sorrows grow'. Old Montague professes himself 'willing' to 'give cure' to his son's unhappiness and is relieved when Benvolio offers to take it upon himself – 'know [Romeo's] grievance, or be much denied'. Benvolio's concern for his cousin suggests affection and anxiety for Romeo that stretches into the wider family. The Montague family's genuine concern for their youngest son contrasts sharply with the dictatorial and business-like approach taken towards Juliet and her future by the Capulets.

The closeness of the Montague family is underscored by the impact of Romeo's exile in Act III. After Mercutio – kinsman to the Prince – has died by Tybalt's hand and Tybalt too by Romeo's, Old Montague pleads urgently for his son's life. He reminds the furious Prince that Romeo was 'Mercutio's friend' and 'his fault concludes but what the law should end,/ The life of Tybalt'. The Prince, grudgingly, takes this into account and banishes Romeo from Verona instead of allowing the Capulets to demand his death too as 'blood price' for Tybalt's. Nonetheless, Romeo's punishment clearly has a significant impact on his family – even before his eventual, more devastating fate, is discovered. The Montagues' loyalty to one another is exemplified in the servant Balthasar's ongoing support for Romeo throughout his exile and his endeavours to reunite with Juliet. More tragically, Lady Montague's love for her exiled son results in a grief so deep that, Lord Montague tells us in the closing scenes, that it 'stopp'd her breath'. By contrast, Lady Capulet only imagines that the mutual death of Romeo and Juliet might propel her into a 'sepulchre'.

A final point to bear in mind when considering the case for the Montagues being the gentler and kinder of the two warring families is that, despite the losses of his wife and youngest son, Lord Montague shows greater magnanimity when the Montagues and Capulets finally agree to make peace. Lord Capulet is the first to finally reach out, offering his hand as his 'daughter's jointure' – accepting the marriage of Romeo and Juliet as he was unlikely to have done had they survived – but it is Lord Montague who goes one step further, promising to 'raise [Juliet's] statue in pure gold' and ensure that she is remembered throughout Verona as a 'true and faithful' daughter and wife instead of a rebellious child. Old Montague appears determined to ensure the longevity of the houses' newborn alliance by committing a substantial financial sum to a monument to remind them both of why that peace has been made.

But perhaps you disagree. Is Old Montague merely trying to one-up the Capulets in this end scene? Could Tybalt's hot-headed propensity to seek a brawl be interpreted as a different kind of family loyalty? Is Juliet's planned union with Paris designed to provide for her by her protective parents and ensure a far safer future than she gains by choosing to unite with Romeo? These questions are well worth debating.

The Capulets

For a play that revolves so much around family, it's interesting that the word 'family' never appears in the play at all. Instead, Shakespeare chooses to explore the relationships that we find *within* a family. Father and daughter, mother and daughter, nurse and ward. But why, might we ask, do we see so much more of Juliet's family relationships than of Romeo's? What dramatic possibilities did Shakespeare see in this family of a young girl?

Who are the Capulets? They're a noble family from Verona, and Juliet is their only daughter. The only other family member is Tybalt, Juliet's cousin, but servants are mentioned. Lord Capulet has the fourth-longest part in the play after Romeo, Juliet and the Friar, and hosts the party that Romeo crashes, where the two lovers meet. Lord and Lady Capulet both want to see Juliet married - which makes sense given the contextual expectation for nobility to marry young. Tybalt's death sparks a desire in Capulet to get moving more quickly on his daughter's nuptial plans, and the big fallout happens when he tells Juliet that she's being married off on - Wednesday? Not Wednesday! Too soon! Thursday, then. She says no, is disowned by her father and then her mother in quick succession.

Through modern eyes it's easy to see the Capulets as cruel, misunderstanding, even abusive. Juliet's thirteen! Why would they be so determined to see her married so young and within a few days? It would also be straightforward to say 'But it was a different time! We can't judge historical values by today's circumstances!' This section is going to explore the idea that there is a middle ground, and that by looking at Juliet's relationship with her parents we can start to pick apart whether it's possible to see them as more sympathetic than first impressions suggest.

We'll start with Juliet's mother. The first time we see her is in Act I, Scene 3. There's palpable tension between her and the Nurse over who 'mothers' Juliet. It's as if Shakespeare never quite finished casting, leaving both roles up for grabs. From the start, she's not positioned as fully in control as she has to ask the Nurse for her daughter's whereabouts - 'Nurse, where's my daughter? Call her forth to me'. The Nurse is a sort-of gatekeeper, answering Juliet's 'How now, who calls?' with 'Your mother'. Lady Capulet can't quite make up her mind about what role the Nurse is playing in this room, asking her first to 'give leave awhile' and then to 'come back again'. They seem to compete over who knows more about Juliet, as Lady Capulet says 'She's not fourteen', answered by a flurry of *yes, I know!* from the Nurse - 'I'll lay fourteen of my teeth,/ And yet, to my teen be it spoken, I have but four,/ She's not fourteen'.

This all-female environment is quite tense, then. It's what we would call a *homosocial* environment, one where we only see characters of one gender interacting. It means that the first time we see Juliet is in a domestic, familial setting with other women, whereas Romeo is introduced in a more public space. Already, there's a sense that Juliet 'belongs' here in the heart of her family home. Juliet's mother makes a strong link between marriage and children, saying 'Well, think of marriage now. Younger than you,/ Here in Verona, ladies of esteem,/ Are made already mothers'. She does her best to sell the idea of marriage as being literary, godly, spiritual, having its place amongst the greatest aesthetic achievements: 'Read o'er the volume of young Paris' face,/ And find delight writ there with beauty's pen;/ Examine every married lineament,/ And see how one another lends content.' In this speech, the perfect full rhyming and the pointed use of the word 'married' seems a bit try-hard, an attempt to make the language as perfect and as matching as she wants Juliet and the beleaguered Paris to be.

On the other hand, the Nurse's portrayal of marriage is more practical. The Nurse tells us that her daughter Susan died as a child, and that her husband was clumsy, telling us of the earthy humour and innuendo of which Juliet was the subject. Juliet therefore gets two conflicting examples of adult womanhood - one that sees marriage as a goal of beauty, the other that sees marriage as a goal of sex. No wonder, then, that one of the first things that we hear Juliet say is her opinions on marriage. When her mother asks 'How stands your dispositions to be married?' she answers 'It is an honour that I dream not of'. Lady Capulet is portrayed as a character who doesn't have much dramatic space as a mother, pushed out by the length of the Nurse's speeches and fighting to make her language more appealing, more perfectly rhyming than the Nurse's confused and chopped verse. After all, Lady Capulet tries to quieten her employee by saying 'Enough of this, I pray thee, hold thy peace', using the informal or contemptuous 'thou' to address the Nurse. However, towards Juliet she uses the politer 'you', reflecting their nobility and difference in status.

Hopping forward in the play, we can see further examples of both Lord and Lady Capulet positioned as characters who struggle to dramatically 'fit in', and perhaps here is another type of tragedy. In Act III, Scene 5, Juliet and her mother are having parallel, but ultimately different conversations, underscored by the fact that Shakespeare often gives them the same words to repeat.

Capulet's Wife	Well, girl, thou weep'st not so much for his death As that the **villain** lives which slaughtered him.
Juliet	What **villain**, madam?
Capulet's Wife	That same **villain** Romeo.
Juliet [aside]	**Villain** and he be many miles asunder.

Their repeating the word conjures the impression of unity, of understanding, but given that their opinions of the 'villain Romeo' are worlds apart, they merely speak the same word and not the same meaning. We also see that when Lady Capulet says that they'll arrange for Romeo to be killed, and then her daughter 'wilt be **satisfied**', Juliet's answer that 'I never shall be **satisfied** /With Romeo till I behold him' is of a much more sexualised nature. They speak the same words, but the difference in meaning marks disunity and separation.

The most painful moment for Juliet and her parents is the final scene of Act III. Here Capulet casts aside his daughter for refusing Paris' hand in marriage.

The 'salt flood' of Capulet's anger blazes through this section. At first, it seems that Lady Capulet may be goading him to react - 'she gives you thanks./ I would the fool were married to her grave'. However, his anger then overtakes that of his wife's, and she asks him to cool his anger - 'You are too hot'. This whole scene is full of weather imagery: 'When the sun sets, the earth doth drizzle dew'; 'sailing in this salt flood'; 'a sudden calm will overset/ Thy tempest-tossed body'; 'Is there no pity sitting in the clouds/ That sees into the bottom of my grief?'. The first full conversation that we see with both Juliet and her parents is a storm that whips up passions and anger. Capulet's anger is really set off by Juliet's 'chopped logic'. Whereas before he was unhappily enquiring without quite so much unbridled fury - 'Soft, take me with you, take me with you, wife', there is a sense of him becoming lost and confounded in a lack of understanding as he fails to keep up with Juliet's 'logic' and is outwitted, shown up, by her deft turns of phrase. There is no calming of the waters in this scene. Juliet's father leaves alone, and his wife only follows afterwards, again showing that they are not in step with each other.

When Juliet has been found dead - really dead, this time, not in drugged sleep - Capulet turns to his wife and says 'O heavens! O wife, look how our daughter bleeds!' It is a moment of real pain. Linguistically it is simple, and the repetitive closeness of 'O heavens! O wife' emphasises the abject despair. This direct address to his wife contrasts with the disunity that has come before, showing us how the teenagers' deaths have started to knit characters closer together. Just as Lady Capulet has, before, tried to create aesthetically beautiful rhyming phrases, Capulet now turns to the same technique to create a sense of finality, of order imposed on disorder - 'give me thy hand... for no more/ Can I demand'.

Where the Capulets have been out of step with each other, they are now in step, united in grief. They are also, however, in step with the Montagues at the end of the play. There is a poetic beauty in Montague speaking Juliet's name in the final few lines, followed by Capulet naming Romeo. Both families conclude the play by delicately holding the name of the 'enemy' child within a rhyming couplet. Montague says 'There shall no figure at such rate be set / As that of true and faithful Juliet'; Capulet says 'As rich shall Romeo's by his lady's lie,/ Poor sacrifices of our enmity'.

At the start of this essay we suggested that the Capulets can be seen as abusive and cruel. Arguably, they can be presented as victims of a fate more mundane and less performative than two teenagers dying in a disjointed suicide - the fate of always being slightly out of touch until it's too late. Perhaps Shakespeare chooses to explore the Capulets in more depth than the Montagues because of Juliet's relative vulnerability, her youth and more sheltered position. Perhaps it's also because the play gives us a more intimate view of Juliet's passage from child who 'dream[s] not of' marriage to a wife who is prepared to summon the heavens to bring her new husband to her bedchamber, a journey that pits her directly and quickly against her elders. Yet another interpretation would be the fact that without her parents disowning Juliet, she wouldn't set off to fake her own death, meaning that their dismissal enables the tragedy to take place in the way that it is set out in the Prologue.

In any interpretation, it's clear that the Capulets are characters whose disavowal of their own daughter is punished soundly. Capulet's last line notes that the two bodies are 'Poor sacrifices of our enmity'. Perhaps the word 'our' refers to his and Juliet's enmity, as well as that of his family and the Montagues.

Mercutio and Benvolio

Mercutio

Mischievous, moody Mercutio is one of the play's most compelling characters. Restoration poet and playwright, John Dryden declared that 'Shakespeare show'd the best of his skill in his Mercutio'[10] – a statement that is hard to disagree with! Witty and outspoken, Mercutio leaps off the page and stage as a spirited and exuberant figure to the extent that he is sometimes considered to be a dramatic problem by critics; he is a notorious 'scene stealer,'[11] who almost overshadows Romeo. Dryden further notes that Shakespeare himself said 'he was forced to murder [Mercutio] in the third Act to prevent being killed by him.'[12]

A relative of both Prince Escalus and Count Paris, Mercutio is one of the few characters who moves freely between the two warring families. But, ironically, he is often a catalyst for their conflicts. His name is derived from 'mercury', linking it both to the element and the Roman god. The former, otherwise known as 'quicksilver', is commonly found in thermometers and barometers –

---

[10] John Dryden, 'Defence of the Epilogue [to the Second Part of Granada]; Or an Essay on the Dramatic Poetry of the Last Age,' *Of Dramatic Poetry and Other Critical Essays,* Vol. 1, ed. G. Watson, London, 1962, 180.

[11] Raymond V. Utterback, 'The Death of Mercutio,' *Shakespeare Quarterly.*

[12] Dryden, 180.

perhaps alluding to his role as something of a temperature gauge between the two hostile houses – but also is notably toxic, indicating his negative effect on the already sour relationships. Certain traits of the god seem relevant to Mercutio's characterisation too: he is the god of messages and trickery, as shown in his ornate but unstable language – watch out for his switches between prose and metre. Perhaps more importantly, Mercury is also the god of boundaries, known for his role in guiding souls to the underworld. In his ability to instigate fights and, ultimately, his dying curse – 'a plague o'both your houses' – Mercutio fulfils the role of a figure who lives in the betwixt and between and conjures people over to the other side.

Despite his energy and intensity, though, there is something curiously powerless about Mercutio. He has parallels with some of Shakespeare's 'stage-director' characters, such as Rosalyn in *As You Like It*, Cleopatra in *Antony and Cleopatra,* and Prospero in *The Tempest*, because he often endeavours to direct the actions and speech of other characters, and is conscious of his own theatrical role. 'Men's eyes were made to look, and let them gaze,' he exclaims in Act III, Scene 1, demonstrating both awareness of and disregard for the audience he compels both within and of the play - 'I will budge for no man's pleasure.' Perhaps because of his lack of interest in what his audience might desire, unlike his aforementioned counterparts, his attempts to command others' performances often fail.

In Act II he speaks in incantations outside the Capulet orchard, demanding Romeo 'appear'. But only darkness and silence follow. It is Benvolio who sees and 'speaks' Romeo into being when they meet by chance a few scenes later. Mercutio is also chided by his friends for making his 'tale[s] large' and for 'lov[ing] to hear himself talk'; such comments suggest he is prone to exaggeration and fibs, rather than someone whose voice has authority within his immediate circle. Curiously he is also rule-bound, showing shock when Romeo refuses to answer Tybalt's challenge to a duel. When his attempt to shame Romeo into the fight – 'O calm, dishonourable, vile submission!' – also fails, he ends up acting the part his friend refuses, taking it upon himself to fight instead.

Despite his larger-than-life depiction, it is Mercutio's own death that generates the greatest action from others within the play. It is in response to his murder by Tybalt that Romeo casts off what Mercutio sees as his love-induced 'effemina[cy]' and finds his 'fire-eyed fury.' Spurred to action, Romeo kills Tybalt. The Prince, too, escalates his penalties for the feuding families, banishing Romeo and imposing on the Capulets 'so strong a fine/ That you shall all repent the loss of mine'. Mercutio's death, then, acts as a turning point in the play, pivoting it from a perilous attempt to forge new familial bonds between the hostile houses to certain tragedy.

Dryden himself disagreed with Shakespeare's assessment of Mercutio, and personally 'saw nothing in him but what was so exceeding harmless that he might have lived to the end of the play, and died in his bed, without offence to any man.'[13] Given Mercutio's penchant for mockery, the likelihood of his giving offence to no man [or woman, judging by the Nurse's annoyance with him!] seems slight. But his life within the play is, in many ways, far less significant than his death.

Benvolio

Lord Montague's nephew and Romeo's cousin, Benvolio is another character whose purposes are often thwarted. His name translates as 'good will' or 'peacemaker', but his attempts to 'keep the peace' are uneven at best. When he enters in Act I, Scene 1, he does so to 'part these men' – squabbling servants of the Montagues and Capulets – but is quickly drawn into a swordfight by the hot-headed Tybalt and classed among the 'enemies to peace' by the infuriated Prince. Similarly, in Act III, his efforts to encourage Mercutio to 'retire' when 'the Capels are abroad' in the hope of 'scap[ing] a brawl' prove futile and he has no more success in staving off disaster than Romeo does for refusing Tybalt's challenge.

---

[13] Dryden, 180.

Perhaps more noteworthy in Benvolio's character is his 'good will,' illustrated by his unswerving support of his friends and his consistent use of measured words and judgement. He is trusted within his own household to provide an honest account of events in the first clash of families at the play's opening. Despite his family connections, he is similarly trusted by the Prince to provide a true description of the 'bloody fray' between Mercutio, Tybalt, and Romeo in Act III.

His language, while less effusive than Mercutio's, is no less eloquent. When he describes the servants' quarrel to Old Montague, he speaks of 'the servants of your adversary, and yours,' the careful placement of Old Capulet's servants first implicitly laying blame on the other household while stopping short of saying 'they started it' and tactfully reminding Old Montague that his own servants were there too and 'close fighting'. This all-but-even distribution of responsibility is reinforced by his references to 'more and more' who fought on 'part and part'; the use of the same words ['more' and 'part'] to describe both households deliberately denies any distinction between them and suggests each was as bad as the other.

Benvolio's thoughtful language is mirrored in his thoughtfulness towards his friends. When Lady Montague asks after her son in Act I, Scene 1, Benvolio explains he has seen Romeo but 'gladly shunn'd who gladly fled from me' since he recognises that his friend needed to be alone with his thoughts. He acts similarly when Romeo disappears into the Capulet orchard, despite Mercutio's attempts to taunt him back again. He is just as sensitive to Mercutio when he attempts to persuade his friend to avoid the Capulets. Emma Torrance has noted Benvolio's focus here 'on the influence of the weather and the Capulets' presence rather than his powerful friend's wild, reckless personality'.[14] As with his description of the servants' fight, he deliberately displaces potential blame elsewhere to avoid infuriating his social superior, whilst simultaneously indicating that they too will be implicated since 'we shall not scape a brawl'.

---

[14] Emma Torrance, 'Character Analysis: Benvolio, Mercutio, and Tybalt in Romeo and Juliet,' *Discovering Literature: Shakespeare and Renaissance*, British Library.

While a less magnetic character than Mercutio, Benvolio is far from short of wit. His wordplay with Romeo when he seeks to discover the initial cause of his cousin's distraction [Rosaline] is swift and playful, parrying Romeo's gloom with gentle humour and probing past his deliberate obfuscations. Unlike, Mercutio, however, his quick tongue is rarely cruel or provoking. Instead, he serves as a steady counsellor and mediator for his friends, standing by them through both mental and physical upheavals. His character's greatest weakness is akin to that of Friar Lawrence's; he seeks to create peace where it is unlikely to be found. It is, we must recall, Benvolio who encourages Romeo to attend the 'ancient feast' of the Capulets to enable him to 'compare [Rosaline's] face with some I shall show/ And...make thee think thy swan a crow'. While he is successful in transferring Romeo's affections away from Rosaline, this is the least wise of his decisions as it sets in motion not only the 'star-cross'd' love story but also the grounds for Tybalt's challenge in Act III.

Some critics consider Benvolio and Mercutio to be foils to one another, with reliable Benvolio casting Mercutio's dangerous character into sharp relief. What do you think? Is Mercutio a provocateur or powerless? Is Benvolio a peacemaker or does he, in his own way, also stir up trouble?

Other Characters

Prince Escalus

Verona's prince is a man deeply weary of the disturbance caused by the hostile houses of Montague and Capulet. His three appearances in the play are all triggered by fresh conflicts between the two houses, of which he must determine the cause, the culpability, and the penalties. We see little of his character beyond that, on each occasion, he serves as detective, judge, and jury. These roles that he seems to fulfil fairly. In the aftermath of each quarrel, he listens to each house's version of events and, as we see most  clearly in Act V, weighs these against other pieces of evidence such as the witness statements of Friar Lawrence, Balthasar, and the Page, as well as Romeo's letter to his father to decipher the truth before reaching his verdict. His penalties for each new brawl also increase in severity as the violence escalates throughout the play. Arguably, however, the Prince is too patient with the warring clans and suffers as much as they do as a result. Confronted with the deaths of Romeo and Juliet, he chastises Old Montague and Old Capulet for the fatal results of their ongoing feud but also himself since he 'for winking at your discords too/ Ha[s] lost a brace of kinsmen'.

If we look to the prior quarrels in the play, we can quickly see that the Prince tends to tread too softly rather than clamp down on the clans' hostilities. In Act I, he threatens 'torture' and pain of death' if the sparring servants, Benvolio, Tybalt, and the Old Lords do not 'throw [their] mistemper'd weapons to the ground'. He promises too that 'if ever you disturb our streets again,/ Your lives shall pay the forfeit of the peace'. Simultaneously we learn, however, that this is already the third such disturbance of Verona's streets and the third time that Verona's 'ancient citizens' have been moved to 'part your canker'd hate'. It raises the question as to why the Prince – knowing the historic enmity between the two houses – has not threatened such consequences before.

His concern for his citizens is, moreover, is not sufficient for him to really punish the clashing clans. The quarrel in Act I concludes with little more than a verbal rebuke for each house. It is not until the fourth fight in Act III results in his kinsman Mercutio's death – when 'my blood for your rude brawls doth lie a-bleeding' – that he really takes action. He steps up his penalties for the families to a financial punishment, telling the Montagues and Capulets that he will 'amerce you with so strong a fine/ That you shall all repent the loss of mine'. Note, though, that he still goes back on his word and does not take any lives in 'forfeit of the peace'. Romeo's life is spared in favour of banishment. Had the Prince taken stricter action here, he might have saved himself the loss of another kinsman – Paris – who dies at Romeo's hand in Act V.

When exploring the Prince's character, you might want to think about whether you agree that he is too soft on the Montagues and Capulets early on and whether some of the play's misfortunes might have been prevented with more severe consequences for any of the previous civil brawls. You might also want to discuss whether the Prince and the Law are the same thing – look particularly at Old Montague's plea for Romeo's life on the grounds that his killing of Tybalt 'concludes but what the Law should end' in contrast to Lady Capulet's claim that only Romeo's death with suffice as compensation for Tybalt's. Is the Prince weak or fair? Is he ultimately responsible for not preventing the escalating violence between the two houses, or a man bound by the limits of the law that his subjects determinedly flout?

Friar Lawrence

Friar Lawrence is introduced to us via an oxymoronic soliloquy, ostensibly about the natural world's ability to heal and destroy in equal measure. His

words, however, are often read as a metaphor for human nature and, we might argue, his own. The Friar's proclaimed ambition is to 'turn [the Montague and Capulet] households' rancour to pure love'. Often he is depicted by critics as wise and insightful, capable of looking beyond the perhaps fleeting affections of the young lovers to the potential for their marriage to bring peace and benefit to all Verona. We should not forget, however, that his actions contribute to Romeo and Juliet's deaths, so much so that in our present day he might even be considered guilty of manslaughter. It is he, after all, who marries them in secret – against the rules of his religious order and pushing at the boundaries of civil law. It is he too who encourages Juliet to pretend to agree to a marriage to Paris and then to fake her death, instead of confessing to her parents that she is already wed and trusting the Prince to resolve the situation. If the Friar's behaviour is meant to be that of an ally to the young lovers, he is at best naïve in believing that years of enmity can be erased by an illicit marriage.

But is the Friar's behaviour indeed well-intentioned? Scholars of Shakespeare might recall another Friar – the disguised Duke in *Measure for Measure* – who exploits the very person he professes to support, the young nun Isabella, as part of a bigger political scheme. *Romeo and Juliet*'s Friar might likewise be driven by more self-serving, personal goals. Franciscan Friars travelled and preached in the streets, living in church properties in extreme poverty, and were dependent for survival on the charity of communities. Given the widespread impact of the Montagues and Capulets' feud on Verona's streets and citizens, a Friar who contributed to establishing a permanent peace would likely benefit personally from such an outcome. If the Friar is less interested in helping Romeo and Juliet than he is in securing his own rewards, it would go some way to explaining why he is prepared to overlook Romeo's propensity to 'dot[e]' on women and 'waver' in his affections and trust his claim to love Juliet. It also makes sense of his cowardly flight when he finds Romeo dead in the tomb when Juliet awakens.

Before we condemn the Friar as a self-serving villain, however, we may want to consider his confession in Act V. In particular, his willingness to 'let my old life/ Be sacrificed' 'if aught in this miscarried by my fault' weighs in his favour. Had the Friar's plans worked out, the 'death' of Juliet would have served as a metaphor for the destructiveness of the feuding family's hate. Thereafter the joy brought about by her revival in Romeo's arms would lay the grounds on which to heal the breach between the families. Perhaps the worst the Friar is guilty of is being too romantic.

Paris

County Paris is kinsman to Prince Escalus and would-be suitor to Juliet Capulet. Although the play sets up the Montagues and Capulets as mutual antagonists, it is Paris who is Shakespeare's primary villain.

As a competitor for Juliet's love and, like Tybalt, a man who will not allow Romeo to walk away from a fight he does not want, it is easy to see how Paris is positioned as another antagonist for the Montagues. More interesting,  however, is his relationship with the Capulets. The Capulets identify enough qualities in Paris to make him worth considering as a suitable husband for Juliet. He is deemed a 'valiant' man by Lady Capulet and, most importantly, one sufficiently high in status and well off that, if Juliet agrees to 'share all that he doth possess,' she will 'mak[e herself] no less'. A match with Paris, from her parents' perspective, will ensure her a good future in terms of status and financial security.

Despite these pragmatic advantages, the Capulets do not seem wholly at ease with the budding arrangements. Paris appears to be pressuring Old Capulet when he appears for the first time in Act I, Scene 2, since Old Capulet answers his suit with a reminder of what he has 'said before', that Juliet is 'yet a stranger in the world' and he would prefer to 'let two more summers wither in their pride/ Ere [h]e may think her ripe to be a bride'. Despite this, Paris presses on until Old Capulet concedes that he can 'woo her' and seek 'her consent', before he will then validate the match. Paris does not fulfil his end of the bargain, yet he continues to pressure the Capulets to progress the marriage in Act III despite the recent loss of Tybalt. It is this that catalyses the rift between Juliet and her parents, driving her to the desperate measures to reunite with Romeo that result in her death.

It is difficult not to see Paris, as Juliet does, as a 'toad'. Toads were an early modern symbol of poison according to Edward Topsell in his *Historie of Serpents* [1608], as they were widely believed to be 'most venomous.' While such a metaphor is rather hard on the toad as a species, the perception that frogs and toads could 'creepe into' any houses despite the inhabitants best efforts to be rid of them, polluting everything that they touched, is a fairly accurate description of Paris' effect on the Capulet household. Juliet's swallowing of the sleeping draft given to her by Friar Lawrence thus becomes an act of self-poisoning to escape the poison spread by the toad-like Paris.

Tybalt

The fiercest, most hot-headed of characters, a self-proclaimed hater of peace, permanently on the cusp of violence, always spoiling for a fight, the irascible, choleric leader of the Capulet gang, Tybalt is a character the audience might struggle to identify with, like, or, indeed, understand. On top of his other unappealing, hostile characteristics, his killing of the entertaining Mercutio is both pointless and ignoble - stabbing his adversary when he is unable to defend himself. We might even feel that justice is served, that Tybalt gets what he deserves, when Romeo kills him in revenge for his friend's murder. Tybalt is the play's angry young man, a foil to showcase Romeo's more appealing version of youthful masculinity.

Can a case be made, however, for Tybalt as a victim as well as a perpetrator of violence, as a victim of the gang-like, feuding atmosphere, the fetishization of weapons and the toxic masculine culture of Verona? In his own warped perceptions, Tybalt is a staunch defender of his family honour, his readiness to fight a testament to both his skill and courage. Keen to test his mettle, he is intoxicated by the thrill of the fight and seduced by the glamour of weapons. But mostly, fighting has been only a dangerous game for him, a sport, until with Mercutio's death, it suddenly becomes all too horribly real. He is also the leader of the young Capulets and when the crunch comes, as such, he has to take the lead in any fighting. He is loyal and bold and carries out the only role he thinks he is required to play. Such dangerous, warped and immature perceptions – he is only, after all, a young man - have been moulded by the world around him, by his forefathers and those in power. His behaviour may seem, indeed is, rash, wild and dangerous, and we may not, in all good conscience, be able to label him simply as a victim, but we don't have to look too far in our own culture to see many mini-Tybalts.

GLOSSARY

ALIENATION EFFECT – coined by German playwright, Berthold Brecht, it reverses the conventional idea that audience's suspend their disbelief when watching a play

ANTITHESIS – the use of balanced opposites, at sentence or text level

APOSTROPHE – a figure of speech addressing a person, object or idea

ASIDE – brief words spoken for only the audience to hear

CADENCE – the rise and fall of sounds in a line

CATHARSIS – a feeling of release an audience supposedly feels the end of a tragedy

CONCEIT – an extended metaphor

DRAMATIC IRONY – when the audience knows things the on-stage characters do not

FIGURATIVE LANGUAGE – language that is not literal, but employs figures of speech, such as metaphor, simile and personification

FOURTH WALL – the term for the invisible wall between the audience and the actors on the stage

GOTHIC – a style of literature characterised by psychological horror, dark deeds and uncanny events

HAMARTIA – a tragic or fatal flaw in the protagonist of a tragedy that contributes significantly to their downfall

HEROIC COUPLETS – pairs of rhymed lines in iambic pentameter

HYPERBOLE – extreme exaggeration

IAMBIC – a metrical pattern of a weak followed by a strong stress, ti-TUM, like a heart beat

IMAGERY – the umbrella term for description in poetry. Sensory imagery refers to descriptions that appeal to sight, sound and so forth; figurative imagery refers to the use of devices such as metaphor, simile and personification

JUXTAPOSITION – two things placed together to create a strong contrast

METAPHOR – an implicit comparison in which one thing is said to be another

METRE – the regular pattern organising sound and rhythm in a poem

MONOLOGUE – extended speech by a single character

MOTIF – a repeated image or pattern of language, often carrying thematic significance

ONOMATOPOEIA – bang, crash, wallop

PENTAMETER – a poetic line consisting of five beats

PERSONIFICATION – giving human characteristics to inanimate things

PLOSIVE – a type of alliteration using 'p' and 'b' sounds

ROMANTIC – a type of poetry characterised by a love of nature, by strong emotion and heightened tone

SIMILE – an explicit comparison of two different things

SOLILOQUY – a speech by a single character alone on stage revealing their innermost thoughts

STAGECRAFT – a term for all the stage devices used by a playwright, encompassing lighting, costume, music, directions and so forth

STICHOMYTHIA – quick, choppy exchanges of dialogue between characters

SUSPENSIOIN OF DISBELIEF – the idea that the audience willing treats the events on stage as if they were real

SYMBOL – something that stands in for something else. Often a concrete representation of an idea.

SYNTAX – the word order in a sentence. doesn't Without sense English syntax make. Syntax is crucial to sense: For example, though it uses all the same words, 'the man eats the fish' is not the same as 'the fish eats the man'

TRAGEDY – a play that ends with the deaths of the main characters

UNITIES – A description of tragic structure by Aristotle that relates to three elements of time, place and action

WELL-MADE PLAY – a type of play that follows specific conventions so that its action looks and feels realistic.

About the authors

A member of Ofqual's Experts panel for English, Neil Bowen is an experienced Head of English, a writer and an editor. Neil has a Masters Degree in Literature & Education from Cambridge University and is the author of 'The Art of Writing English Essays' for GCSE, co-author of 'The Art of Writing English Essays for A-level and Beyond', as well as The Art of Poetry & Art of Drama series. Neil runs the peripeteia project, bridging the gap between A-level and degree level English courses www.peripeteia.webs.com, and regularly presents at conferences. Recently he has also started to run his own CPD sessions for English teachers and tweets @neilbowen3.

Having been awarded a first-class honours with a Dean's Commendation from the University of Exeter, Dr Briony Frost completed her PhD thesis on Jacobean Drama and politics. A regular seminar leader for the peripeteia project, Briony has lectured in English Literature at Plymouth and Exeter Universities and is currently working at the University of Bath.

Johanna Harrison is currently studying for an MA in Modern Literature and Culture at King's College London, having completed her undergraduate study in English Literature at Oxford University. She also holds a postgraduate degree in Music from the Guildhall of Music and Drama.

Alice Penfold is the Assistant Subject Leader for English and Reading Coordinator in a secondary academy. She completed her BA in English Language and Literature at Oxford University and has since completed a Master's in Children Literature. Currently she is working on a PhD, focused on representations of mental health in young adult fiction.

Jennifer Webb is an English Teacher and the Assistant Principal for Teaching, Learning & Staff Development at. In the past she has worked as a Head of English, Lead Practitioner and an AST in a number of schools in West Yorkshire. Jennifer is a best-selling author ['How to Teach English Literature: Overcoming Cultural Poverty' & 'Teach Like a Writer'], speaks at conferences both home and abroad, regularly delivers CPD, and is interested in challenge and aspiration in inner-cities. She writes a widely read T&L blog [funkypedagogy.com] and tweets @FunkyPedagogy.

Printed in Great Britain
by Amazon

64782578R00068